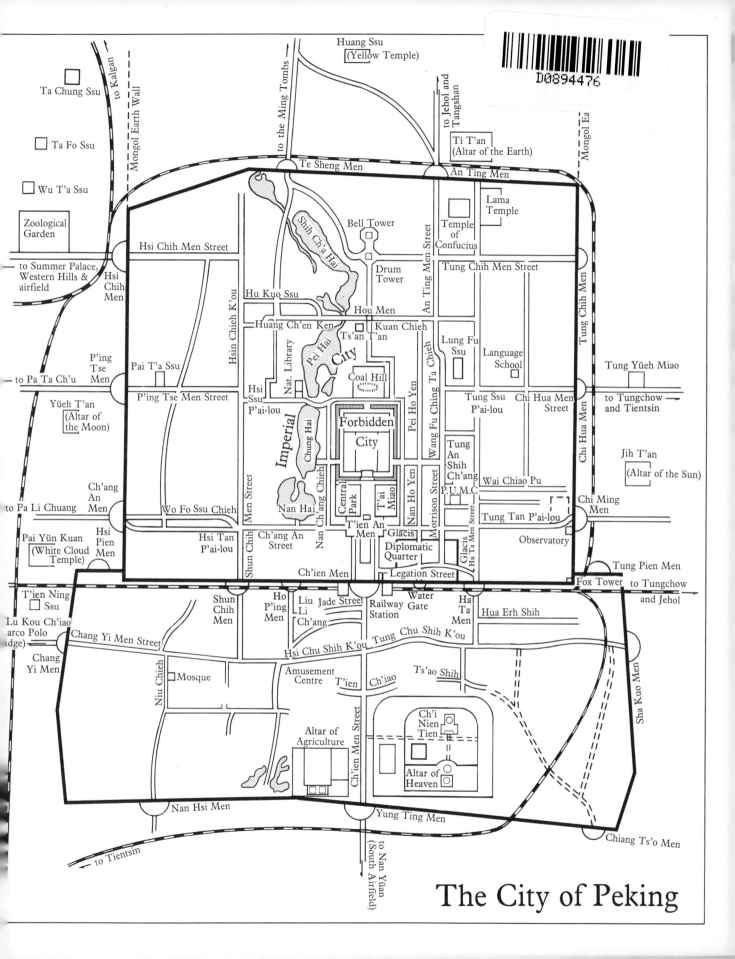

The City of Peking

A PHOTOGRAPHER IN OLD PEKING

A PHOTOGRAPHER IN OLD PEKING

Hedda Morrison

With a Foreword by Wang Gungwu

HONG KONG OXFORD NEW YORK
OXFORD UNIVERSITY PRESS
1985

Oxford University Press

Oxford New York Toronto
Petaling Jaya Singapore Hong Kong Tokyo
Delhi Bombay Calcutta Madras Karachi
Nairobi Dar es Salaam Cape Town
Melbourne Auckland

and associated companies in
Beirut Berlin Ibadan Nicosia

First published 1985
Published in the United States
by Oxford University Press Inc., New York

Library of Congress Cataloging-in-Publication Data
Morrison, Hedda.
A photographer in Old Peking.
Bibliography: p.
1. Peking (China)—Description—Views.   I. Title.
DS795.M84 1985   951'.156   85-29764
ISBN 0-19-584056-9
ISBN 0-19-583974-9 (pbk.)

Designed by Rosanne Chan
Printed in Hong Kong by Golden Cup Printing Co. Ltd.
Published by Oxford University Press, Warwick House, Hong Kong

To the memory of
Henry Vetch

Foreword

I FIRST met Hedda Morrison when she had just produced an excellent volume of photographs about Sarawak. This was on the eve of the formation of Malaysia and, for those of us living in Kuala Lumpur, her pictures were a vivid and illuminating introduction to a new member-state of the Federation. When we talked, she spoke of her beginnings as a photographer in China and her professional life in Peking between 1933 and 1946. Having seen her work on Sarawak, I expected her pictures of China to be equally good but, in her usual modest way, she described them as a beginner's efforts. It was not until many years later that I saw a few of her Peking photographs. I was struck by their beauty and each one of them is still etched in my memory. I did not realize then how many she had taken and how consistently memorable they were until she showed me the collection she had put together for this volume. Now it is with great delight that I commend them to everyone who appreciates the art of photography.

As an historian, I would go even further. Peking is one of the great cities of the world and we cannot have too many pictures of it. Even more poignant is the fact that it has been so changed during the past thirty years that the city's marvellous past is in danger of being lost to memory, becoming merely the stuff of nostalgia. Thus every bit of it that reminds the historically minded of what the city used to be like is a valuable document. By that criterion, this is a volume of significant documents, all the more significant because they are the work of one of the finest photographers who has ever worked in Asia. The volume stands as a great memoir of Peking from 1933 to 1946 and of the varied life of the people who were privileged to live in it, each of the photographs saying more to us than can be conveyed in a thousand words.

Canberra
August 1985

Wang Gungwu

Contents

Introduction

I KNEW very little about China when the opportunity arose for me to go there in 1933. The opportunity was in the form of an advertisement in a German photographic journal for a qualified woman photographer to manage Hartungs Photo Studio in Peking. The advertisement was almost tailor-made for me since it specified a Swabian — natives of Swabia are reputed to be hard workers — able to speak English and French. My home town was Stuttgart and I had the necessary language qualifications. I had recently completed my studies at the Munich Photo School, followed by work with a distinguished and demanding photographer by the name of Lazi. I was anxious to work overseas, as I had no sympathy for the Germany of the time, and the idea of working in far-away Peking greatly appealed to me. The salary was modest — that was why a woman was sought for the job. I was to find that the work was very hard, the hours being from seven o'clock in the morning to six o'clock in the evening six days a week, with unpaid overtime whenever special work had to be completed quickly.

However, it was a decision that I was never to regret though at the time my family had some misgivings. Their parting gifts were a pistol for my personal protection and an umbrella, both of which I dropped overboard as soon as I left Trieste aboard an Italian liner. The intention had been for me to travel trans-Siberia but this route was closed because of the Japanese invasion of Manchuria.

I was to remain with Hartungs until my contract ended in 1938. Thereafter I worked for several years for an English lady, Miss Bieber, who had long been resident in Peking and was interested in Chinese arts and crafts. For most of the time I lived in a small section of the Chinese residence of the French Consul, Jean-Pierre Dubosc, an authority on Chinese painting. His charming wife was the daughter of Mr C.T. Loo, a well-known antiquarian who resided in Paris. The house was in Nan Ch'ang Chieh between the Forbidden City and Nan Hai.

I was able to see a great deal of Peking and to travel modestly — as one could in those days — to a number of places of interest in north and central China. I left China in 1946 after my marriage. My husband was born in Peking and worked in the British Embassy from the end of 1940 until the outbreak of the Pacific War. Life in China was followed by a long residence in Sarawak.

The Peking that I came to and where I had the management of a large photo studio and its staff of seventeen Chinese men was in the twilight of its days as a centre of the old China. The city had become the capital of China in 1421 during the reign of the Ming Emperor

Yung Lo. It was the last of several cities built on the site, its importance lying in its strategic position commanding the routes to Mongolia and Manchuria. In 1933 the great walled city, its gateways and the outer moat were still largely intact and well maintained. Its population, though reduced from its heyday, numbered more than one million people.

Peking was the last of the great Chinese imperial capitals. It had seen the decline and decay of the imperial system and it had twice been captured by Western armies, in 1860 and 1900. After the latter, at the time of the so-called Boxer Rebellion and the siege of the foreign legations, the city had been savagely looted both by the Boxers and by the invading forces. The Boxer Rebellion was the violent anti-foreign and anti-Western movement that engulfed much of north China at the turn of the century. Though partly a popular movement, it also enjoyed the support of the court. It culminated in 1900 with widespread massacres of Christians and attacks on the foreign missions in Peking which were relieved after a siege of eight weeks in August 1900.

Subsequently the foreign missions established their own walled quarter within the city, complete with crenellated walls and a glacis and saps. Near the British Embassy a section of the original legation wall was preserved, pock-marked with bullet holes and bearing the words 'Lest We Forget'. All the important foreign missions, apart from the German, still had their own military guards.

After the revolution which overthrew the Manchu dynasty in 1911 and established the Republic of China in the following year Peking became a prize to be argued about and fought over by contending Chinese politicians and warlords. But in 1928, after the rise to power of General Chiang Kai Shek, the capital had been moved to the more central location of Nanking in the Yangtze Valley. With the exception of Germans, who lost the status after the First World War, foreigners enjoyed extra-territoriality, which meant that they were subject to the laws of their own country when in China.

Relations with Western countries were moving into a more enlightened phase in the thirties but Western threats to the integrity of China had been replaced by the much graver threat posed by Japan. The Japanese first quarrelled with China over Chinese domination of Korea which Japan subsequently annexed. They had destroyed Russian power in the Far East in the war of 1904–5 and after the First World War they had gained effective control of formerly German-controlled Shantung. Shortly before I arrived in China the Japanese had seized the north-eastern provinces of Manchuria and established the puppet government of Manchukuo. They maintained a large military presence in China; their businessmen were active everywhere, and many had been resident in Peking for a considerable length of time.

Yet Peking retained its unique character. As a centre for education and the arts, much of the old way of life and the old craft skills continued. Within its great walls innumerable small roads and lanes called *hu-t'ung* ran north-south and east-west in accordance with Peking's symmetrical plan. If you gave or received directions they were always in terms of the compass: go north, take the second turn to the east, and so on.

The buildings, with the exception of a few Western-style offices and public buildings, were single-storied, made of grey brick and roofed with grey tiles. The walls enclosed family courtyards; the gates of the well-to-do were painted an auspicious shade of bright red. You could not see into the houses because within the gates there was usually an inner spirit wall facing the gate and round which one had to pass on entry. This wall was intended to hinder the entry of evil influences. From any vantage point it was difficult to imagine that you were in a great city: the trees planted in the family courtyards gave the city a rural appearance punctuated only by the golden roofs of imperial palaces and temples and by the imposing gate towers in the city walls.

At the centre of Peking lay the Forbidden City, once the opulent palace compound of the Chinese emperors but in the thirties largely open to the public. Surrounding the Forbidden City was the so-called Imperial City, in which had lived the high Manchu officials. West of the Forbidden City lay a series of lakes and pleasure gardens, the whole encompassed by the high walls of the Tartar City originally reserved for Manchu troops. South of the Tartar City, and linked to it by lower walls, was the Chinese City where the Manchus had required ethnic Chinese to reside, a restriction which had long since broken down. Within its confines the Chinese City housed most of the business areas but was far from fully occupied and contained considerable areas of farmland.

Throughout the city and outside the walls were dotted great monuments to the religious life of the old China. Some temples were in poor repair and some had seriously deteriorated, but most were open to the public. Many retained endowments of land or support from worshippers which enabled maintenance of a kind to continue. The majority of the seriously damaged temples were those which had been used as temporary troop quarters.

Religion played an important role in the life of the old China but in bewildering variety. While the great temples of the major faiths, especially Taoism and Buddhism, were particularly noticeable to the foreign visitor, religion was far from confined to these large centres of worship. There existed as well a great body of folk religion and animism with its roots deep in the past. Religious life was also influenced by the philosophical precepts of Confucianism, and by a reverence for ancestors so profound as to merit the term 'ancestor worship'. In addition Christianity and Islam had made a considerable impact on China.

Taoism, 'the religion of the way', which had both monastic and secular forms, had probably the largest number of followers. It originated with the philosophical writings of Lao Tzu in the sixth century BC but later developed into a popular religion with an elaborate pantheon and the life of Lao Tzu himself mightily embroidered into a fanciful mythology. The pantheon was elaborate because it was open ended. Anyone who had rendered meritorious service to mankind could be deified after death. There was a god or goddess, or both, to watch over almost every human interest, trade or profession. The Taoist sought immortality through meritorious deeds. There was also a widespread belief that one could gain eternal life through medication and dieting and by the use of magical elixirs. The religion imparted social stability because it taught that there would be heavenly retribution for misdeeds on earth. The Chinese being practical people, there was even a scorecard available in the form of a Taoist handbook which enumerated 1,230 good and bad deeds with the quantum of good and bad marks set down for each entry. The Taoists believed that the Kitchen God oversaw the doings of each family on earth and that he recommended rewards and penalties annually to the Great Jade Emperor God. Temples contained dramatic representations of what might happen to both the good and the bad in the next world.

Much more is known about Lao Tzu's contemporary, Confucius, who was a distinguished official and philosopher. His teachings were not religious, making no mention of the salvation of the soul or the life after death. Confucius was concerned with the enunciation of a system of morality and ethics which would provide the basis for good government. He called for filial piety and family cohesion, courtesy and social stability, diligence at one's calling, and the recognition of the importance of agriculture. His teachings are embodied in the classical text entitled *The Analects,* which, together with several other classics and commentaries on them, formed the syllabus for entry by public examination into the imperial civil service. There was a magnificent temple in Peking dedicated to the memory of Confucius, and I was fortunate to be able to visit his birthplace in Shantung where some of his descendants were still living.

Buddhism was introduced to China from India in the first century AD. The faith was sympathetically received and gained many adherents and much imperial patronage. Buddhists sought to achieve the state of Nirvana, the complete merging of the soul into the spirit of the universe through the annihilation of desire and by following the eight-fold path of right belief, right resolve, right word, right act, right life, right effort, right thinking and right meditation. The Mahayana Buddhism practised in China differed considerably from the Theravada Buddhism of South-east Asia. The latter doctrine stressed monastic asceticism, whereas the former was more liberal and accommodated a number of benevolent bodhisatt-vas — beings who are on the way to, or already worthy of, Buddhahood but who have chosen to remain on earth to help others achieve salvation.

In Peking there were also temples devoted to the Lamaist form of Buddhism. This had evolved in Tibet as an amalgam of Indian Tantric Buddhism which laid stress on magical practices and the old indigenous faiths of Tibet involving shamanism and the worship of various benevolent and demonic spirits. Lamaism was not only the faith of Tibet but also of the Mongols and Manchus.

At the same time the Chinese worshipped their ancestors. Although this was basically a matter of paying respect to ancestors and was accepted as such by the early Jesuit missionaries to China, the ceremonies and practices involved had been influenced by Taoism and Buddhism.

The religious life of ordinary people largely involved worship of the Taoist gods, but simultaneously there was a universal and more ancient veneration of natural objects, of heaven and earth, the sun, moon and stars, mountains and rivers, and natural phenomena of many kinds. There were tree gods and flower nymphs, as well as dragon kings in charge of seas, rivers, lakes and wells. There was an elaborate system of geomancy, *feng-shui,* designed to harmonize the location of residences and tombs with cosmic currents. This often entailed the building of shelter walls or embankments or putting bends in roads, which might more conveniently have been straight, in order to deflect unfavourable influences.

In north China certain animals such as the fox, the marten, the hedgehog, the snake and the rat, were held in reverence. The fox and the marten were family gods of fortune and small shrines were often erected to them. Hedgehogs and snakes were respected but were also bad omens and to be avoided. Rats were benevolent because they were capable of bringing to their worshippers great riches from other families. And the bat, generally an object of revulsion in the West, was, though not actually revered, a symbol of happiness.

An underlying concept was that of Yang and Yin, the principle of complementary opposites that governs the universe and everything in it. The old Chinese philosophers perceived duality everywhere: heaven and earth, male and female, sun and moon, positive and negative, light and darkness, and so on. Heaven, the male positive element, light, the dragon, odd numbers, the colour blue, all were Yang. Earth, the female passive element, darkness, the tiger, even numbers and the colour orange were Yin. Everything in nature was either Yang or Yin.

Islam had come to China overland from Central Asia and by sea to the ports of south China. There were, and still are, large numbers of Muslims, the Hui people, in western China, and other communities exist in most large cities. In Peking there were several mosques, and Muslims were prominent as restaurateurs.

Christianity had at one time gained great influence in China through the remarkably gifted and energetic Jesuit missionaries who first arrived in China at the end of the sixteenth century. The Jesuits were learned and cultivated men of rare ability, were held in high respect in China and gained great influence at the imperial court. They adopted a tolerant attitude towards the Chinese practices, respecting Confucius and the veneration of ancestors. This accommodation aroused the strong opposition of the more bigoted Dominicans and Franciscans who were also allowed to proselytize in China. The Vatican eventually pronounced in favour of the latter early in the eighteenth century. This in turn annoyed the Chinese and, although the Christian orders were able to carry on missionary activities, the churches were subjected to much persecution and never regained the position of respect and sympathy acquired by the Jesuits. When the great influx of Christian missionaries arrived in China in the nineteenth century they were often regarded by the Chinese as part of the Western impact on the country and associated with the political expansionism of Western powers.

Initially Peking had served as the capital of the Ming emperors but in the seventeenth century the Ming were overthrown by the non-Chinese Manchus from Manchuria. The last Ming emperor committed suicide in Peking in 1644. Although the Manchus had their own language and script they rapidly assimilated Chinese culture, and life in China went on much as before. The great Manchu emperors of the seventeenth and eighteenth centuries brought exceptional peace, prosperity and unity to China. Decline set in during the nineteenth century when internal divisions and corruption, the impact of the West, intense conservatism and the inability to adapt to a changing world set imperial China on a path of irremediable decline.

Apart from the growing Japanese population there were quite a number of foreigners in Peking when I arrived there. Although the capital had moved to Nanking most Western countries still maintained a presence in Peking. There were diplomats, missionaries and academics, legation guards, a business community and a small floating population of those attracted by the charm of Peking and the comfortable and interesting life that could be enjoyed there. The cost of living was low and residents could expect to be looked after by extraordinarily accomplished servants. These servants were small businessmen who, in return for a modest wage and a commission levied whenever possible on anything that their employer purchased for his own sustenance or acquired for his pleasure, undertook to see that he was well cared for. In particular the Chinese cooks of foreigners in Peking had an exceptional mastery of the art of Western cooking.

Peking was a reasonably healthy place for Europeans provided they drank boiled water and saw to it that any vegetables to be eaten raw had been well washed. However, considering the small size of the European population, sudden deaths were more common than one might have expected. I knew one woman who died of rabies contracted from a playful kitten. A Danish friend was killed by carbon monoxide poisoning from the stove in his bathroom. The British Consul in Peking who in 1946 performed the civil marriage ceremony for my husband and myself contracted meningitis on the very eve of his own wedding and died a few days later.

But underlying the charm of Peking and the hedonistic life that could be enjoyed there, lay much hardship and grinding poverty. Beggars were not a true reflection of poverty as many were professionally organized. It was the people who did not beg who reflected the most extreme poverty. No means of earning a living, whether by scavenging for paper and rags or collecting grasshoppers for bird keepers in the summer months, was neglected. And people died of exposure on the winter streets. What was most remarkable was the uncomplaining and cheerful fortitude of those who endured great hardship.

The winters were very severe. There was little snow for Peking has a very dry climate, but there was thick ice on the lakes for several months. Cutting ice from the lakes and moats and preserving it underground for use in the summer constituted a minor industry. The main source of heat was coal, most of which came from small collieries in the Western Hills. From there it was transported to the city largely by camel trains.

Most Chinese houses had no general heating but had raised brick benches called *k'ang* through which air passages conveyed hot air from a stove outside the room. In European houses and those of well-to-do Chinese a type of central heating was provided by iron stoves, the flues from which ran long distances before emerging to the outside air. The coal for these stoves would be delivered direct to the house by camel. For cooking purposes coal balls containing a large proportion of clay were commonly used.

A disagreeable feature of Peking was the frequency of dust storms, especially in the early spring. It was said that the dust came all the way from the Gobi Desert in Mongolia but actually it was simply whipped up from the arid, deforested landscape of north China. It is interesting to note that the Chinese had long since learned to use translucent paper in their windows as a means of keeping out the cold air.

Dust storms apart, spring was delightful, but the hot summer months were oppressive and this was when the rains fell. The best season of all was the autumn. At all times of the year the light, except during dust storms, had a brilliant quality which the old Chinese architects had exploited to the full in their use of coloured roof tiles for important buildings, especially the golden roof tiles of the great imperial palaces.

Life in Peking was not only visually pleasing but there were also many sounds which appealed to the ear. All kinds of goods and foodstuffs were hawked through the streets and *hu-t'ung*. Each kind of hawker had his own particular clapper or gong or trumpet, generally coupled with a melodious cry. Wedding and funeral processions always had their own bands of musicians. Street entertainments, of which there were many, had musical accompaniments. Some of the fine Chinese songbirds, especially the *pai-ling* (Mongolian Lark) and the *hua-mei* (Spectacled Laughing Thrush), were kept for the beauty of their songs. Even the stridulation of crickets was appreciated. Crickets would be kept in tiny cages in which they stridulated all summer long until they died at the onset of cold weather. The Pekingese also kept many lofts of domestic pigeons. Strapped to the base of their tails the pigeons had lightweight bamboo instruments which produced a rather mournful flute-like note when the birds were released from their lofts to circle over the city.

Even at night Peking had its own distinctive sounds. On a quiet night the tock-tock of the night watchmen's wooden clappers was a common sound as the men made their rounds through the *hu-t'ung*. It was hardly an efficient way to protect householders from wrongdoers but no doubt people slept the more soundly as a result. Actually there was little serious crime in Peking and personal security was of a high order. If property was stolen and if you found your stolen property for sale in a shop — as once happened to me — you were expected to buy it back, but the shopkeeper could be expected to let you have it for a reasonable price.

I spent my leisure time exploring the city and its neighbourhoods, generally by bicycle. It was impossible to be bored in Peking as there was so much to see and to photograph, and everywhere I was treated with the greatest courtesy and consideration. I found the people to be willing and obliging photographic subjects, treating my requests with good humour and patience. Having photographed many hundreds of Chinese in every walk of life, I cannot recollect a single instance when a request to photograph was rebuffed.

Patience was required, because in those days before electronic flash I often had to pose people and ask them to keep quite still. The only flash I had in Peking was an elaborate contraption made for me by a German friend which used the rubber bulb of an old-fashioned car horn to puff magnesium powder over burning Meta fuel. It emitted an enormous flash and was useful when photographing dark interiors. It was also dangerous and I once set myself aflame when photographing the Ming frescos of a temple in the Western Hills. The lack of reliable flash equipment is the reason for the small number of photographs of domestic interiors.

In the past the first glimpses of Peking when you arrived by train from Tientsin were the high walls and the city gate at the south-east corner of the Tartar City. The railway ran along the south side of the wall to the terminus just outside the great central gateway, Ch'ien Men. Outside there was little motor traffic on the broad roads. There were some horse-drawn carts and many bicycles and rickshaws, small man-drawn carts. In the old China human labour provided the cheapest and most abundant source of power, and so the rickshaw was a universal form of transport. There was also limited public transport: a few buses and a network of old-fashioned foreign-owned trams which clanged and rattled their way along the chief traffic arteries of the city.

Throughout the year many traditional festivals were still observed in Peking. These followed the old Chinese calendar, a modified lunar calendar, which runs about one month behind the Western calendar. The most important festival of the year was the celebration of the New Year which generally fell in February. Preparations went on for some time before. The poster of the Kitchen God, his face smeared with a little sugar, was sent off in a bonfire to report on the doings of the household to the Jade Emperor God. Red paper decorations with auspicious phrases written on them were pasted on the doors, as were new posters of the Door Gods. Special dumplings were prepared in the form of a tael, the old Chinese silver piece. All debts had to be repaid. Workers normally received a bonus of one month's salary but only a few days' holiday which was their only holiday of the year.

The New Year itself was ushered in with the discharge of many fire crackers. There was much feasting. Temples were visited and family calls made. There were many New Year markets. An especially interesting one took place in Liu Li Ch'ang in the western part of the Chinese City. This was an antique dealers' fair patronized by all the leading dealers in paintings and other art forms. There was a great deal of gambling.

These celebrations were followed on the fifteenth day of the first moon by the Lantern Festival, when shops and private homes hung up elaborate lanterns and many were given to the children. Some shops displayed lanterns made out of blocks of ice. The New Year celebrations ended with a so-called Devil Dance at the Lama Temple where Tibetan scriptures were read and dances were performed by lamas adorned with ferocious masks.

At the end of the second moon came the festival of Ch'ing Ming (Clear and Bright) which falls about the same time as Easter. It was above all a time when Chinese visited and tidied up their graveyards, paid respects to their ancestors and burned much paper money. This was thought to be converted automatically into real money for use in the next world. Sweeping and tidying up of graves also took place in the seventh and tenth moons.

On the fifth day of the fifth moon, in early June, the Dragon Boat Festival was held. It marks the summer solstice but derives its popular name from the regattas held in south China at this time. The long boats with prows carved to represent a dragon's head were powered by many paddlers, who paddled in time to a beating drum. The festival was not extensively celebrated in Peking but once again was a time for settling debts.

A particulariy picturesque celebration occurred on All Souls Day, on the fifteenth day of the seventh moon. Again family graveyards were visited and in the evening little floating lanterns were set adrift on lakes and other stretches of water to help guide lost souls to deliverance. Thirty days later came the Mid-autumn Festival, a home festival for the worship of the moon and a time for family reunions. On this occasion special moon cakes were exchanged and eaten. It was again a time for settling debts.

These were only some of the more important festivals. The endless round of festivals and ceremonies and fairs which could be participated in by rich and poor alike provided the old China with an extraordinarily strong framework for happy social activity.

I was fortunate to be able to make many excursions from Peking. Even with very limited means it was possible to travel widely. I visited most of the important temples of the Western Hills, the mountainous country that covers a large area to the west of the city. I spent one summer holiday with three donkeymen and three donkeys visiting the so-called Lost Tribe country, an area of the further Western Hills where rebellious soldiers had been settled long before. A curious feature of this area was that the old and regrettably brutal Chinese practice of foot binding — deforming girls' feet — had been forbidden here in imperial times and commenced only after the revolution when the practice was being abandoned in the rest of China.

Two other trips took me to Jehol, the former imperial summer residence north of Peking, and another took me to the Yün Kang caves in Shansi. Especially memorable was a visit to the sacred mountain of Hua Shan in Shensi where precipitous peaks are topped by a series of picturesque Taoist temples. The Taoist priests made me most welcome, and even dressed me up as a priest so that one of their number could photograph me with my own camera. In Shantung I travelled along the coast in a Chinese boat from Wei Hai Wei to Tsingtao. I later visited the sacred mountain of T'ai Shan in the same province and Ch'ü Fu, the birthplace of Confucius, and contracted scarlet fever on the journey. I also spent some time in Nanking to take the photographs for a book on the city by the German scholar Alfred Hoffman and published in Shanghai just before the end of the Second World War. Much of old Nanking had been destroyed during the T'ai P'ing rebellion in the 1850s but it was still a beautiful city. More recently, in 1937, the city had been brutally ravaged by the Japanese.

Most of my travel was done alone and I never felt in any way insecure. Chinese attitudes towards a solitary woman traveller could not have been more correct and helpful, and I met with courtesy wherever I went.

Although the change of environment involved in moving from Germany to Peking was very great, I never felt a stranger in China. On arrival I knew very little about China. My relations with the Chinese staff were pleasant but there was a process of mutual adjustment. It is not easy for Chinese men to work under a European woman, but we established a harmonious relationship and I like to think that I enjoyed their respect and goodwill. The only other European photo studio belonged to a Russian by the name of Serge Vargasoff, who was an excellent, though not very businesslike, photographer. We enjoyed a firm friendship and it was he who brought me the news of the Japanese surrender — and a bottle of vodka with which to celebrate the event.

The customers included many interesting personalities. Some became good friends and through them I met many other people. Amongst them I remember with special affection Henry Vetch, the proprietor of the French Bookstore in the Peking Hotel. His shop was a Peking institution. It contained a magnificent stock of books on China, and Vetch was also very active in publishing a whole series of excellent works on the country. He had a fine mind, was a man of enormous energy and a tremendous talker. His wife was a cultivated, kind and patient Russian lady. I used to accompany Vetch and his children and various friends on many of his Sunday walks in the Western Hills. He allowed me to borrow any books that I liked from his shop. When the Communists occupied Peking he at first wrote warmly of the new order but he soon fell foul of Chinese suspicions and was imprisoned for several years. But he never gave up hope, nor did his wife who remained in Peking throughout his imprisonment. He bombarded the Chinese authorities with well reasoned submissions in excellent Chinese and was eventually released. He entertained no rancour at his treatment and continued his publishing career as actively as ever in Hong Kong until his death in 1978.

Père Teilhard de Chardin often came to Hartungs and later I used to meet him at the house of Jean-Pierre Dubosc as he and Dubosc were close friends. Teilhard was a most charming man and a brilliant scientist in the great tradition of distinguished Jesuits who have made their mark in China. He was very much a man of the world and had a long-standing relationship with a gifted American sculptress. It came as a surprise to me to learn later on of his distinction as a religious thinker and mystic.

After I left Hartungs I took many photographs for the English writer, Harold Acton, who spent most of the thirties in Peking. He especially studied the Chinese theatre and I photographed many actors for him. He often entertained actors to dinner after performances and I was sometimes invited to attend, an unusual privilege since I was always the only woman present.

Mr Bill Lewisohn, co-author of the excellent book, *In Search of Old Peking,* gave me much good advice on travel in the Western Hills about which he had an encyclopaedic knowledge. Another writer was the American George Kates, who was the author of a charming work on Peking, *The Years That Were Fat,* and of a comprehensive study of Chinese furniture for which I took the photographs. I was befriended by Adam von Trott who was later to lose his life through his involvement in the plot on Hitler's life. Von Trott was in Peking when my contract came to an end, and I wanted to stay on in China. My employers, fearing that I would set up a rival business, wanted me to return to Germany. They brought considerable pressure to bear on me through the German Embassy and refused to give me the terminal payment that I was due. I never asked Adam von Trott to act for me, but hearing of my problems he took up the cudgels on my behalf. As a consequence I was able to remain in China and received half the payment due to me.

I also met a good many journalists. Outstanding was a dynamic Swiss lady called Lili Abegg. She outstripped all her male colleagues in energy and enterprise when covering the Lu Kou Ch'iao incident and its aftermath in 1937 which triggered off the Japanese attempt to subjugate China. She borrowed my rucksack and set off for forward areas while most of the men were busily looking for news in the Legation Quarter.

Another Hartungs customer was the explorer Sven Hedin who was in China in about 1936 with a large retinue to make what must have been his last visit to Asia. Together with the Hartungs cinematographer, Mr Lu, I accompanied Hedin, then very elderly and something of a prima donna, to the Ming tombs to take some film.

Most of the Hartungs customers were very pleasant and considerate people who used to recount their experiences, show me their photographs and ask for my advice. Inevitably there were exceptions, and strangely, although my relations with Americans have nearly always been good and although I have had many American friends, all the most disagreeable experiences involved well-to-do Americans. A particularly shameful episode occurred at the end of the war when I had no work and was extremely hard up. An American academic wearing the uniform of a US army colonel asked me to take a technically difficult set of photographs of a little-known work in the Forbidden City. This I did in the bitterest cold. I was never paid, even for the materials, nor could I obtain any redress.

After I left Hartungs my work with Miss Bieber involved helping her to adapt Chinese jewellery and silverwork for costume jewellery and to produce embroidery for use by Westerners. Miss Bieber had original ideas and excellent taste but could not manage a working relationship with Chinese. She also required assistance when visiting the various markets to buy the Chinese jewellery she needed to incorporate in costume jewellery, and the Chinese toggles (small pendent ornaments which are the equivalent of Japanese netsuke) which she collected. On these occasions I was often struck by her hard bargaining. She was a wealthy woman but often turned down unique opportunities to buy fine things for considerations which were financially trivial. She left Peking in 1940 for the United States and never returned. Her collection of Chinese toggles, now in Chicago, has been described by Dr Schuyler Cammann.

Life became difficult after the outbreak of the Pacific War. I had been lucky to have invested all my small savings in an order for films and photographic paper in 1941 which arrived by rail from Germany just before the route was closed as a result of the German invasion of the Soviet Union. But my stock of materials eventually ran out. French officials and their families were moved into the Legation Quarter and I lived on alone in the Dubosc compound. One thing I was never troubled by was lack of electricity though there were frequent blackouts for much of the city, nor did I ever have any electricity bills. It was only after some time that I discovered from Dubosc's caretaker-watchman that the electricity supply had been connected to the house next door which was occupied by a senior Japanese official who never suffered from blackouts.

When the war ended Peking was at first occupied by US marines fresh from the campaigns in the Pacific. After a time I was lucky to be given work by the American Red Cross which looked after the welfare and entertainment of the men, and which was housed in the Italian Embassy compound. I was treated kindly, and helped to prepare a small guide to Peking. I also became an expert at serving ice-cream in the Post Exchange.

I was given various assignments which called for local knowledge. One of the most surprising was the request to produce a camel on which marines could be photographed riding. It was midsummer. Finding a camel was by no means easy because camels were usually sent back to the cool grasslands of Mongolia for the summer. However, I eventually located a female camel which had been too pregnant to manage the long walk back to Mongolia. She was duly transported, together with her young one, in a large military truck to the Italian Embassy. Here, despite her protests, she was thoroughly vermifuged before the photographic session was allowed to proceed.

On another occasion I was mildly reprimanded for making a group of marines walk too far on a tour that I had taken to the site of the Old Summer Palace. I remember especially a US army photographer called Eddie. He was a good photographer and very fond of beer — he always had some handy when working in his darkroom. One day I received an agitated telephone call from Eddie seeking urgent advice. Given the task of developing some films for VIP visitors he had inadvertently developed a VIP film in lager. Nothing could be done to repair the damage.

My residence in Peking finally came to an end in the autumn of 1946.

Throughout my stay in Peking Rolleiflex twin lens reflex cameras (alas made no more) were my main standby. In my opinion there has never been a better camera. Many architectural and some other studies were taken with a 9 × 12 cm Linhof Satzplasmat camera. A few photographs towards the end of my stay were taken with a Makina 6 × 9 cm camera.

Walls, Palaces and Parks

THE walls of Peking were some forty kilometres long. Varying between nine and twelve metres in height and pierced by sixteen gateways, each topped by a tall tower, they stood as a striking monument to the grandeur of China's imperial past. There were many other walled cities in China and in other parts of the world, but there has never been anything to compare with the walls of Peking.

There were two main sections of city wall. The northern part of Peking was the so-called Tartar City originally reserved by the Manchu rulers for use by fellow Manchus only. It was roughly square in shape, the walls some twelve metres high and with nine gateways. Three of the latter opened on to the southern section of Peking, the Chinese City, where the Manchus had required Chinese to live. This was rectangular in shape, wider but narrower than the Tartar City. Much of its northern wall consisted of the southern section of the Tartar City wall. The remainder of the Chinese City wall, though still impressive, was a mere nine metres in height. It had seven gates leading out of Peking.

The walls were built of brick, and were visible from afar, their battlements and towers standing out starkly above the flat North China plain. Together with an outer moat these walls had originally played an important defensive role but they presented no great obstacle to the modern weapons of Western powers in 1860 and 1900. The walls were retained for another half century, partly because of ingrained Chinese conservatism and partly because they were useful in maintaining internal security. But in the eyes of modern Chinese developers they had no useful role to play and were therefore removed.

Adjoining the eastern wall of the Tartar City and built on a section of an earlier wall, was the Astronomical Observatory. Astronomy was an advanced science in China at an early period of history. Further advances were made on the arrival in China of the early Jesuit missionaries, men of science who introduced Western theories on the subject. The observatory housed some magnificent instruments, some purely Chinese and some built to French designs by Chinese craftsmen. Many of the finest ones had been taken as loot by the German occupying forces at the time of the Boxer Rebellion but were returned to China after the First World War.

When I was in Peking the walls and gates were still in a fair state of repair. Walking was permitted on many sections of the wall. Here, high above the city, one could walk for miles and disturb only a few goats browsing on the bushes and rough grass that had grown up there. On the moat side were many duck farms, and in the winter ice blocks were cut out of the moat for use the following summer. On the city side lay houses and courtyards and small factories and many open grassy areas and some cultivated land. The horizon was broken by the golden roofs of the Forbidden City, and by the many other architectural features of old Peking such as dagobas and gate towers, and the tall Bell and Drum Towers north of the Forbidden City.

The Bell and Drum Towers lay to the north of the main central gateway of the Tartar City, Ch'ien Men, a huge structure with twin gate towers. These were in fact of quite recent construction, the originals having been burned down during the Boxer troubles and rebuilt in subsequent years. Nowadays there is a vast open space between Ch'ien Men and the Forbidden City capable of accommodating the world's largest parades and rallies. Before the revolution of 1949 much of this area was built on and contained many Chinese banks and other business houses.

Facing on to the broad east-west thoroughfare, Ch'ang An Chieh (Eternal Peace Street), was the splendid T'ien An Men (Heavenly Peace Gate). Several other gates in Peking also featured the word 'peace' at a time when Western countries tended to name streets, gates and railway stations after military victories. Imperial decrees were read from T'ien An Men but its use as a reviewing stand did not come into being until after the revolution of 1911. In imperial times Wu Men, the front gate of the Forbidden City proper, was used for this purpose. Most of the buildings of the Forbidden City and the walls of T'ien An Men were painted dull red, the balustrades were of white marble and the roof tiles were yellow, the imperial colour.

In front of T'ien An Men was an ornamental canal lined with marble balusters and crossed by five marble bridges. There were two immense guardian lions in white marble and two elegant marble winged pillars known as *hua-piao* (flowery sign posts), and inside the gate was another pair. The *hua-piao* were capped with small lions. The lions on the outer *hua-piao* had their mouths open signifying that it was their duty to report malpractices to the emperor. Those on the inside had closed mouths to indicate that silence was required regarding the emperor's private life.

Before the revolution of 1949 T'ien An Men was a generally quiet place where trees had been planted to give shade and where a few hawkers sold refreshments to visitors and passers by.

T'ien An Men was actually outside the moat and the high walls of the Forbidden City proper. From T'ien An Men a long paved way flanked by guard-houses led to the true front entrance, the massive Wu Men. This in turn gave access to a beautifully proportioned courtyard crossed from east to west by a curving moat, also lined with marble balustrades and crossed by five marble bridges. At the far side of the courtyard was another splendid gate, T'ai Ho Men (the Gate of Supreme Harmony). For the newcomer to Peking the first glimpse of the magnificence of the Forbidden City was best gained from one of the two side entrances to this great courtyard. Walking up a ramp from the outside with no inkling of what was to come, one suddenly came upon this vision of vast open space, enclosed by red walls, white marble and golden roofs.

The roof ridges of the buildings in the Forbidden City and of almost all other important buildings in Peking were surmounted by small figures made as integral parts of the terminal ridge tiles. The lowest figure represents an early tyrant of the year 283 BC who, for his misdeeds, was strung up at the end of a roof ridge and left to die. He is portrayed riding a hen which is afraid to fly down to the ground because of the weight on her back and which is prevented from retreating up the ridge by various animals and a large and fierce-looking open-mouthed monster.

T'ai Ho Men was reached by twin staircases, between which was a great slab of fine marble carved as a dragon. This arrangement was repeated on the far side of this gate and again in the next courtyard which led to the central T'ai Ho Tien (the Hall of Supreme Harmony). The emperor in his sedan chair would have been carried over the dragon, the carriers using the flanking steps.

The next courtyard was immense and completely bare, though in imperial times it would often have been filled to capacity with officials and troops on great state occasions. At the northern end, on a three-tiered marble terrace, stood T'ai Ho Tien and two other ceremonial halls. This was the hub of the empire. The triple staircase was flanked by eighteen great bronze urns representing the eighteen provinces of imperial China. On the terrace stood two bronze cranes and two bronze tortoises, representing longevity and strength. T'ai Ho Tien was the largest of the three ceremonial halls. It was a colossal building, its roof supported by immense lacquered wooden pillars, each one made from the trunk of a single tree.

This great succession of formal courtyards and halls occupied only the central portion of the Forbidden City. To each side of them was a maze of lesser throne rooms, shrines, formal gardens and domestic quarters which constituted the town inhabited by the emperor, his wives, concubines, children, girl servants and a great army of eunuchs, many of whom held high official positions. The eunuch profession was a respected one in imperial times, and large numbers were required for the service of the emperor and princely Manchu households. A Chinese family might decide that one of the sons should become a eunuch much in the same way as a European family might have a son take holy orders. It was not, of course, a practice that was confined to Asia. Until the early nineteenth century in Italy singers for church choirs were commonly castrated.

On each side of the southern entrance to the Forbidden City were to be found two additional important institutions. On the western side was Central Park, originally the Altar of Land and Grain, which had been established as a public park after the revolution of 1911. Exactly corresponding to Central Park on the eastern side was T'ai Miao containing the shrines to the imperial ancestors. The buildings of T'ai Miao date from the fifteenth century, and in them were kept the memorial tablets of the imperial ancestors and of some other important personalities of the Manchu period.

The emperor came to T'ai Miao five times a year to pay his respects and to offer sacrifices. These ceremonies were performed in the three main halls which were situated on a marble terrace surrounded by an inner, walled enclosure. The latter in turn was contained in a large outer precinct in which grew avenues of gnarled and ancient cypress trees and which was bounded on the north side by the moat of the Forbidden City. It was a place of extraordinary charm and tranquillity. It the morning local residents used the precincts to do their *t'ai-chi* exercises, the slow rhythmical exercises that improve bodily coordination and balance, and blood circulation. A curious feature of T'ai Miao was that it contained a large heronry, the nesting place of several species of herons and egrets. After the revolution of 1949 T'ai Miao became the Workers' Cultural Palace.

On the northern side of the Forbidden City lay an artificial hill capped by five small pavilions. This was Coal Hill, formed out of the spoil excavated from the adjoining moat and lakes, and designed to protect the imperial palaces from malign influences coming from the north. On Coal Hill stood a tree from which the last Ming emperor was said to have hanged himself in 1644. From the central and highest pavilion one commanded a beautiful view south over the yellow roofs of the Forbidden City. In the thirties few Western-style buildings obtruded on the skyline.

Still further north, on the same north-south axis leading from Ch'ien Men through the centre of the Forbidden City, were two important towers, the Bell and Drum Towers. These too had a part to play in protecting the palaces from malign influences and spirits. The Drum Tower is thirty metres (ninety-nine feet) in height, the precision a matter of importance since it was believed that only good spirits could rise above that height.

To the west of Coal Hill lay Pei Hai (North Lake), the northernmost of three artificial lakes around which the emperors built a remarkable assortment of temples, lesser ceremonial halls, pleasure gardens and pavilions. The entrance to Pei Hai lay between Coal Hill and a very beautiful marble bridge between Pei Hai and Chung Hai (Central Lake) immediately to the south. At each end of this bridge stood one of the many *p'ai-lou*, or ceremonial arches, which spanned a number of important streets and crossroads in Peking. They were highly ornamental but hardly compatible with modern traffic conditions. They have nearly all been removed.

The lake margins supported great lotus beds which flowered profusely during the summer. During the winter the lakes froze over and were used by skaters. In north China skating is an ancient recreation, which was encouraged by the Manchus. One of the star performers when I was in Peking was an old man who in his youth had performed for the pleasure of the Empress Dowager and her court.

The most conspicuous feature of Pei Hai was a high artificial hill crowned by a white Tibetan-style dagoba, built in 1651 to commemorate the first visit by a Dalai Lama to Peking. From the base of the dagoba one gained another splendid view over the city.

Pei Hai was a favourite resort of the Empress Dowager, even during the Boxer Rebellion when the nearby Catholic cathedral was under siege. The cathedral and the many missionaries and Chinese Christians who had taken refuge there were defended with great gallantry by a handful of French marines. The defenders were sometimes given a little respite when the Empress Dowager ordered firing to cease because it gave her a headache during her picnics on the lake. One of her favourite dishes on such occasions – buns stuffed with minced pork – was still purveyed by one of the many restaurants which had taken over some of the pavilions. In the early morning the Pei Hai grounds were a favourite resort for Chinese actors who did voice projection exercises against some of the pavilion walls and practised their parts in the quiet of the imperial pleasure gardens.

One feature of Pei Hai (and also of the north gate of the Forbidden City and of Central Park) was a collection and hatchery of fine goldfish. Goldfish, derived from a species of carp, had been evolved in China by the eleventh century AD. Many of the varieties were grotesque, with long veil tails, telescope eyes or enlarged heads, but their production showed great skill on the part of Chinese fish fanciers. The goldfish were kept in large earthenware tubs. Gravid females and cock fish would be removed to special breeding tubs before spawning and then returned to their original tubs. The various types of minute fry were kept carefully separated. As well as the hatcheries in the old imperial buildings there was a large commercial fish farm near the Altar of Heaven. Goldfish were hawked through the streets or could be bought at markets, and fish tubs, the best of which were made in Soochow, were a common feature of Chinese courtyards. Supplying valuable fish with live water fleas was the basis for a minor summer industry in Peking, great numbers of water fleas being available in the many canals and ditches.

Chung Hai was a long, narrow sheet of water leading to the smaller, circular Nan Hai (South Lake). In early spring Chung Hai in particular was the haunt of extraordinary numbers of wild duck of many species. As with Pei Hai the lake precincts contained many shrines, pavilions and formal parks. On the west side of the lakes there were also some modern offices and official residences.

On Nan Hai there was an artificial islet on which stood a number of particularly beautiful pavilions. Here the Emperor Kuang Hsü was confined by his aunt the Empress Dowager after the collapse in 1898 of the reform movement which he had supported. It had been the Emperor's intention to confine his aunt there but the plans were betrayed and the Empress Dowager struck first.

The southern entrance to Nan Hai was actually through a pavilion erected by the Emperor Ch'ien Lung for a famous Muslim beauty, Hsiang Fei, the Fragrant Concubine. Hsiang Fei was the wife of a Muslim chief of the western border regions. Her husband took his own life after suffering defeat at the hands of the Chinese, whereupon the Emperor ordered that the beautiful Hsiang Fei be brought to him in Peking. He was much smitten by the lady, heaped favours upon her but was unable to gain her affections. Hsiang Fei also eventually committed suicide after receiving an ultimatum from the mother of the Emperor, during a temporary absence of the latter from the palace, that she must either submit herself to Ch'ien Lung or take her own life.

All the lakes were fed by waters flowing from the Jade Fountain to the west of the Summer Palace. They entered the city at the north-west corner of the Tartar City. Between the entry point and Pei Hai was yet another lake which was not reserved for imperial use, but which had a number of temples and important residences. It was a popular recreation area with many tea houses, and there used to be a foundry in the north-west corner where bells were cast in Ming times. By the thirties all that remained was a spirit wall carved with dragons and made from a great slab of brown stone resembling iron.

A corner of the Chinese City wall.

A distant view of Hsi Chih Men in the north-western corner of Peking
after a fall of snow.

City gate after snowfall.

Ch'ien Men, the central southern gate of the Tartar City, taken from
near the railway station. The small horse-drawn cabs were rarely to be seen
in the latter years of my stay in Peking.

Scene within a city gate.

Frozen moat from which ice blocks were cut
for storage underground and use in the summer.

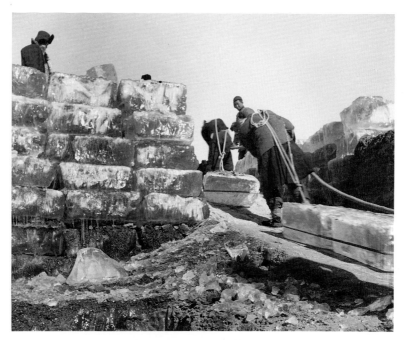

Ice blocks being moved for storage.

Duck farm below the city wall.

Persimmon vendor outside T'ien An Men, the outer gate leading to
the Forbidden City. Persimmons were a cheap and abundant fruit, often kept until they
shrivelled under the winter frosts and became deliciously sweet.

Hua-piao outside T'ien An Men. There was one pair
of these pillars outside and one pair inside T'ien An Men, as
a reminder to the emperor to walk in the path of virtue.

Wu Men, the great front gate to the Forbidden City.

The large courtyard beyond Wu Men and through which runs
a moat spanned by five marble bridges. On the far side
of the courtyard was yet another impressive gate, T'ai Ho Men.

T'ai Ho Tien, the first of three great halls of state which constituted
the nucleus of the Forbidden City, as seen from T'ai Ho Men.
The eighteen bronze urns which stand on the three-tiered marble terrace represent the
eighteen provinces of the empire. Bronze cranes and tortoises represent longevity and strength.
The courtyard is immense but appears somewhat foreshortened in the photograph.

Marble sundial on the terrace of T'ai Ho Tien.

One of four huge gilt-bronze bowls on the terrace.

Coal Hill, the artificial hill lying to the north of the Forbidden City.

The Forbidden City, view south from Coal Hill.

Coal Hill in winter.

A corner of the Forbidden City wall and moat.

The halls of T'ai Miao (the Temple of the Imperial Ancestors), where the emperor
would come at regular intervals to pay his respects to his own forebears.

One of the large carved marble slabs over which the emperor was carried
during his visits to the Temple of the Imperial Ancestors.

The great white dagoba of Pei Hai (North Lake) which was built in 1651
to commemorate the first visit of the Dalai Lama to Peking.

Pavilions at the northern end of Pei Hai.

Roof figures by Pei Hai commemorating the execution
of a cruel tyrant in the year 283 BC.

Detail of glazed tilework by Pei Hai.

The Drum Tower, thirty metres high, which helped protect the Forbidden City from malign influences. In imperial times a drum was beaten here at nightfall.

One of the small pavilions in Nan Hai which was
being used as a private residence.

Spirit wall by Nan Hai.

Nan Hai.

The observatory which adjoined the south-west wall of the Tartar City.

The instruments at the observatory were built by Chinese craftsmen in the seventeenth
century to the designs of the French Jesuit Verbiest.
Earlier instruments designed and made in China had been moved to Nanking.

The Iron Shadow Wall and a water spout in the north-west corner
of the Tartar City. The wall is a solid block of stone but is
said to be impregnated with iron by the foundry which once stood nearby.

Temples and *P'ai-lou*

BECAUSE of the deeply ingrained religious traditions in China, places of worship were to be found everywhere, both in towns and in the countryside. There were temples in even the smallest villages. Temples were generally situated in places of natural beauty and were surrounded by ancient pine trees.

At the pinnacle of Chinese society the emperor was both a temporal potentate and the direct representative of his people in their relations with the spiritual world. Many of the emperor's most important duties involved officiating at regular ceremonies in the great temples of state, while imperial patronage encouraged the building and operation of innumerable lesser places of worship.

In Peking, in addition to T'ai Miao adjoining the Forbidden City where the emperor paid his respects to his ancestors, there were six temples where he, or in one case the empress, regularly undertook religious duties on behalf of the people. Unfortunately several of these temples, and many others, fell on hard times with the decline of the imperial system, and into disuse and disrepair after the revolution of 1911. The temples occupied large areas and were expensive to maintain. Many were therefore neglected or used for other purposes, the worst of all being the use of some as barracks. The process of decay has continued until the present day.

Four great temples of state were sited in complementary pairs on each side of the Tartar City. Each pair comprised the Yang and Yin principle of opposites. In the south, which corresponds to the Yang principle, was the Altar of Heaven. This was the most important of the four and the only one which has been well maintained to the present day. It occupied a huge area in the Chinese City. This was where the emperor performed the year's most important sacrifice at the time of the winter solstice when winter begins to give way to spring.

On the north side of the city was located the Altar of Earth, the Yin complement of Heaven. Here the great annual ceremony took place at the summer solstice after which the days grow shorter and the winter begins to make its approach. The altar was square in shape in conformity with the imagined shape of the earth and contrasting with the circular Altar of Heaven. The roof tiles were imperial yellow as were those of most imperial buildings. Those of the Altar of Heaven were blue, the colour of the vault of heaven.

East of the city was the Altar of the Sun and to the west was the complementary Altar of the Moon. These two were lesser temples and the imperial ceremonies were held only in alternate years at the beginning of spring and autumn respectively. The plans of the two temples were somewhat similar except that the inner walls around the square altars were round in the case of the Altar of the Sun and square in the case of the Altar of the Moon.

Of these great temples of state only the Altar of Heaven has survived intact. When I arrived in Peking it was in poor repair but it was extensively renovated by the puppet government installed by the Japanese after 1937, as were the Forbidden City and a number of other buildings. The altar itself must lay claim to be one of the world's most beautiful man-made structures — three tiers of white marble topped by marble balustrades carved with the representation of clouds, the whole of a refined simplicity and open to the sky. The circular central marble slab produces a booming echo, and the concentric surrounding slabs are all in multiples of nine. The altar is surrounded by an inner circular wall and by an outer square wall with marble gateways at the cardinal points.

The altar was at the southern end of the temple. Immediately to its north was a small, octagonal temple where the tablets of heaven and of the imperial ancestors were kept during the great sacrifice. Sacrifices included a whole bullock, as well as jade and rolls of silk, the two most precious commodities of the empire. This small temple is surrounded by a circular wall of such perfect construction that it had the properties of a 'whispering' wall.

Further north was a great marble causeway leading from the magnificent Ch'i Nien Tien (the Hall of Annual Prayer), a circular building almost thirty metres in height with triple roofs. It is the most conspicuous building in the temple complex but was of minor importance in the celebrations that took place there. It was used at the beginning of spring for prayers and sacrifices seeking a good harvest. Another lesser ceremony took place at the start of summer to seek good rains. Ch'i Nien Tien is a splendid and impressive building but is of comparatively recent construction, as the original building was destroyed by lightning in 1889. Its destruction was regarded as a very inauspicious omen for the Emperor Kuang Hsü whose reign effectively commenced in that year although he had been proclaimed emperor in 1875. And indeed the reign did prove to be a disastrous one for China.

The other three great temples of state were in a state of ruin when I was in Peking and were used for various utilitarian purposes. The Altar of Earth became a public park in 1925 and was later used as an asylum for the insane. The Altar of the Sun was used as a wireless station and for barracks, and the Altar of the Moon was occupied by troops.

Special care was taken by the emperor to seek divine assistance for the all-important processes of agriculture and husbandry. The Altar of Agriculture was situated to the west of the Altar of Heaven. Each spring the emperor would go there to perform a ritual during which he himself ploughed eight furrows and planted rice. Other high officials and aged peasants planted various kinds of millet. Land and grain were the objects of worship at the Altar of Land and Grain at the south-west corner of the Forbidden City. The floor of the terrace on which the altar was situated was covered with earth of five different colours: yellow in the centre, black on the north side, green on the east, red on the south and white on the west. Apart from its agricultural significance the altar represented the integrity and independence of China. Little was left of the Altar of Agriculture when I was in Peking but the Altar of Land and Grain had become the Central Park in 1911 and its precincts had been reasonably well maintained.

At the north-east corner of the Pei Hai enclosure there was an important temple known as Ts'an T'an, devoted to silk culture. It stood in a grove of mulberry trees, where silkworms were raised and sacrifices were offered by the empress during the third moon of each year. Sericulture, the production of silk by raising silkworms, was one of the great achievements of ancient China. According to Chinese legend sericulture was invented in the year 2602 BC. There may be no truth in the legend but it was certainly invented long before the Christian era. From China the process was introduced to the rest of the world.

In terms of precedence the next most important imperial ceremonies after those at the Altar of Heaven took place in T'ai Miao, mentioned in the preceding chapter, but to some extent T'ai Miao could be regarded more as an adjunct of the Forbidden City than as a temple proper. By paying respects to his own ancestors, the emperor was hardly acting as the intermediary between his people and the spiritual world. Other great ceremonies of respect were held at K'ung Miao (the Temple of Confucius) in the north-eastern part of the Tartar City. This was a very ancient establishment dating back to Mongol times and was added to on many occasions over the years. In the thirties it was still the best preserved and best maintained temple in Peking. Here the memory of Confucius and of his ancestors was honoured, especially on the sage's birthday, the twenty-seventh day of the eighth moon. All the leading scholars of the day took part. A feature of these celebrations, which continued for some time after the revolution of 1911, was the playing of ancient music on early types of musical instruments which were stored in the temple.

Adjoining K'ung Miao to the west was another ancient institution, the Hall of Classics. This was founded as a private school in Mongol times but became an élite university under the Ming emperors. In the magnificent central pavilion the emperor himself used to expound the Classics to assembled scholars during the second moon. The texts of the nine classical works which provided the foundation for Chinese learning and conduct were recorded on stone tablets kept in the temple. This was a continuation of the practice of earlier dynasties intended to act as an insurance against any repetition of the mass destruction of books, the infamous Burning of the Books, which had occurred in the second century BC.

There were a great number of other temples both large and small in and around Peking, most of which are detailed in the works of Juliet Bredon, and of Arlington and Lewisohn. Two very fine temples demonstrated the importance to the Chinese of Lamaism, the form of Buddhism followed in Tibet and Mongolia and also by the Manchus. The most important was Yung Ho Kung near the Temple of Confucius. The various buildings contained many figures of Buddhas and of the saints and demons of Lamaism. The imposing central building contains an immense figure of Maitreya, the next Buddha, twenty-three metres in height. Formerly, at New Year, there was a famous ceremony in this temple performed by lamas in brilliant robes and many wearing grotesque masks representing demons. It was known to foreigners as the Devil Dance.

The second important Lama temple, the Yellow Temple, was built on an ancient site outside the north wall not far from the Altar of the Earth. It was built to provide a residence for the Dalai Lama, the ruler of Tibet, who visited Peking in 1652. It was then extended to provide accommodation for the Dalai Lama's staff, and later housed important Mongol dignitaries during visits to Peking. Inside the temple complex was a beautiful marble stupa carved with scenes from the life of Buddha which had been built to honour the memory of a Panchen Lama, second in importance to the Dalai Lama, who died of smallpox in Peking in 1781. By the time I was in Peking the carvings had unfortunately been much mutilated and the temple was in a poor state of repair.

Two great white dagobas which were conspicuous features of the Peking skyline were also Lamaist in nature. One crowned the artificial island in Pei Hai. The other was Pai T'a Ssu (the White Dagoba Temple) in the West City which was virtually all that remained of a once large temple dating back to the Mongol period. It once housed a famous statue called the Sandalwood Buddha, but this was moved to another temple near Pei Hai and disappeared during the Boxer Rebellion.

Also outside the north wall was Wu T'a Ssu (the Five Pagoda Temple), commemorating the visit of a religious personage from afar. This was an Indian known to the Chinese as Pantita who visited Peking in the fifteenth century bringing with him as gifts for the emperor five golden figures of the Buddha and a model of the throne on which Buddha was said to have attained enlightenment. Only the central feature of the temple had survived, a massive square tower capped by five pagodas in the Indian style, the walls of the tower decorated with rows of figures of Buddha. A little to the west of Wu T'a Ssu were two important temples, Ta Hui Ssu (the Temple of Supreme Wisdom), containing a figure of Buddha sixteen metres high, and Ta Chung Ssu (the Great Bell Temple) which featured a colossal bell cast in the early years of the fifteenth century. The bell weighed more than five tonnes.

Many temples were Taoist, the Taoist priests easily recognizable by their distinctive appearance. They wore black gowns and a peculiar hair-style. They did not cut their hair but wore it in a topknot encased in a black hat with a hole in the middle through which the topknot projected, the whole held in place by large pins. The most important Taoist temple was the ancient Pai Yün Kuan (the White Cloud Temple) outside the west wall. It contained many halls and residences and a theatre, and housed a large number of monks. At the time of the New Year it was the scene of a major festival attended by large crowds of visitors. One of the features of the festival was a large representation of a cash (old Chinese coin) suspended below a marble bridge leading over a small canal. If a cash thrown from the bridge hit the large one — a feat that was difficult to achieve — the thrower could be assured of good fortune during the coming year. The collected fallen cash would be contributed to the temple's finances. When cash went out of use the monks, being practical men, opened an exchange booth where currency notes could be converted into the old model currency. A little way south of Pai Yün Kuan was an exceptionally fine Buddhist pagoda, T'ien Ning Ssu (the Temple of Heavenly Peace).

On the eastern side of the city was another large Taoist temple, Tung Yüeh Miao (the Temple of the Eastern Peak). The eastern peak referred to was T'ai Shan in Shantung. The temple was dedicated to one Huang Fei Hu, the reputed killer of a cruel ruler of the Shang dynasty in about 1000 BC. This act having brought peace to the empire, Huang Fei Hu was deified as the supreme god of the sacred mountain of T'ai Shan. The great annual festival at Tung Yüeh Miao to celebrate Huang's birthday in the third moon was attended by crowds of worshippers offering prayers to the special Taoist deities whom they favoured. The temple contained figures of a great number of deities, with one to suit almost every human wish or cause of anxiety: the pursuit of wealth, the desire for children or for a long life, or the fear of illness.

A special feature of the temple were the many groups of figures demonstrating what happens to both the good and the bad in the next world: honourable persons were shown being borne on clouds to paradise, while the punishments in hell for the wicked were gruesome in the extreme. Regrettably this temple no longer exists.

In my later years in Peking I often visited a small Buddhist nunnery in the West City to talk to the nuns and to watch them at their devotions. They were kind women, strangely innocent as to what was happening in the world outside but with a lively curiosity to learn. They used to give me tea and ply me with questions. They were concerned about my own situation and told me that if I ever had difficulties I should come to them for shelter and protection.

Not all the memorials and relics of the past in Peking were associated with religion and the emperor. Some were purely decorative in nature. The most conspicuous of these were the fine archways or *p'ai-lou* which stood at road intersections, at the approaches to many buildings or singly in the countryside. These *p'ai-lou,* rooflets of green tiles carried on great wooden pillars, were generally built to commemorate a famous person or a virtuous deed. In the thirties four *p'ai-lou* still stood at major crossroads in the Tartar City and were much used as direction points. Traffic had to pass under or around them.

Unfortunately the roads of imperial China did not match the beauty of the *p'ai-lou.* Road-building was one of the few arts never mastered by Chinese technology. The roads of Peking and almost everywhere else in imperial times were dirt roads, dusty in dry weather and a sea of mud in the wet. Some important roads were built of solid blocks of stone, but they lacked foundations and through wear, tilting and sinking of the blocks, they soon became extremely rough. Because they were very durable the Chinese said of them that they were 'good for seven years and bad for seven hundred'.

The Altar of Heaven by moonlight. Its three tiers of gleaming white marble
open to the sky, its perfect symmetry and its blend of simplicity and sophistication
make it one of the world's most beautiful man-made structures.
Seen in moonlight it appears to be floating in the air.

One of the four gateways leading to the Altar of Heaven.
This was the most sacred place in the empire and the centre
of the altar was regarded as the hub of the universe.

The Altar of the God of the Universe immediately to the north of
the altar enclosure. Here were placed the tablets of the imperial ancestors
during the great sacrifice at the time of the winter solstice.

Ch'i Nien Tien (the Hall of Annual Prayer), which was linked by a
long marble causeway to the Altar of the God of the Universe.
This striking building, almost thirty metres high and roofed with tiles
of blue, was of minor ritual importance. The present building replaced
an earlier one destroyed by lightning in 1889 at the start of
the disastrous reign of Kuang Hsü, when he reached the age of majority.

The ornate ceiling of the Hall of Annual Prayer.

Detail of one of the pillars of the Hall of Annual Prayer.

The Altar of Agriculture, to the west of the Altar of Heaven. It was the scene
of the ritual spring ploughing conducted by the emperor, high officials and aged peasants.

An interior detail of K'ung Miao (the Temple of Confucius)
where elaborate ceremonies in honour of the sage were conducted, especially on
his birthday, the twenty-seventh day of the eighth moon.

請勿動手

A set of jade chimes, one of the ancient musical
instruments used in the ceremonies honouring Confucius.

The Hall of Classics adjoining the Temple of Confucius and
approached through a triple archway roofed with yellow tiles.

The central pavilion of the Hall of Classics where the emperor used to
expound the Classics to assembled scholars in the second moon of each year.

A young lama from Yung Ho Kung, the Lamaist temple near
the Temple of Confucius. It was originally the site of the palace
of the Manchu prince who became the Emperor Yung Cheng. The palace
of a prince who ascended the throne could not be inhabited again
and so Ch'ien Lung replaced it with the Lamaist temple.

Elaborately gowned figure in the temple.

One of the halls of Yung Ho Kung Lamaist temple.

The stupa of the Yellow Temple which lay outside the north wall of Peking.
The temple was originally built as a residence for the Dalai Lama
who visited Peking in 1651. The stupa was built later, to commemorate
the death of the Panchen Lama who died in Peking in 1781.

The base of the stupa of the Yellow Temple was decorated
with marble panels illustrating the life of the Buddha. Unfortunately
it had been badly defaced over the years.

Wu T'a Ssu (the Five Pagoda Temple) built in honour of an Indian
holy man who visited Peking in 1465 bearing with him precious statues of the Buddha.
Out of respect for his Indian origin the temple was built in the Indian style,
the sides of the square base decorated with rows of figures of the Buddha.

Pai T'a Ssu (the White Dagoba Temple), a prominent landmark of the West City,
which dated originally from 1092 but which had undergone frequent repairs.

Pai T'a Ssu used to house a famous statue known as the Sandalwood Buddha
which was later moved to Pei Hai and then disappeared. While I was in Peking
a small temple in the West City claimed that the statue in the photograph
was the famous figure but this seemed unlikely to be true.

A figure of the Buddha in one of the temples in the West City.

Buddhist nuns in the West City with musical instruments.
They were very devout followers of the Buddha and offered
to provide me with a refuge if ever I needed it.

One of the nuns beating a small wooden drum,
the accompaniment to the chanting of Buddhist prayers.

Pai Yün Kuan (the White Cloud Temple) was one
of the most important Taoist temples in Peking. During a festival
in the New Year period it was thronged with worshippers.

Worship at Pai Yün Kuan involved the burning of much
imitation money in the shape of the old Chinese silver tael, and such
items were sold at the temple during the important festivals.

One of the small pagodas inside Pai Yün Kuan.

A large wooden representation of a cash (old Chinese coin) was suspended
under a bridge in the temple courtyard. If a cash thrown at the representation
hit the target it was a promise of good fortune to come. The cash
thrown were later recovered from the canal and paid into the temple revenues.

A Taoist monk whom I met in Pai Yün Kuan and again later
on the sacred mountain of Hua Shan in central China to which he had
travelled on foot from Peking. As an old acquaintance he took it upon
himself to act as my guide and mentor on Hua Shan.

One of the professional beggars who were always to be seen at temple festivals.

Another famous Taoist temple was Tung Yüeh Miao (the Temple of the Eastern Peak) outside the east wall of Peking. It was renowned for its figures illustrating the rewards and punishments ordained in the hereafter for good and evil deeds in this world.

The Fire God, a large hollow statue filled with burning coal balls
which emitted flames from various body orifices, exhibited at New Year in
another Taoist temple, Ch'eng Huang Miao, in the North City.

One of the many *p'ai-lou* which used to adorn Peking and other Chinese cities. Some commemorated a famous person or a famous deed, and others had a purely ornamental function. They still exist in temples and palaces but have long gone from the roads.

A *p'ai-lou.*

A boy paying respects to his elders and ancestors in a wealthy Chinese home at New Year.

Street Life, Shops and Markets

MUCH of the life of Peking people took place in the streets. Most household essentials were hawked through the streets, each hawker with his distinctive cry accompanied by an equally distinctive clapper or hand gong or trumpet. Some brought entertainment for the children such as puppet shows and performing animals. Itinerant barbers plied their trade and were often to be seen. Under the Manchu dynasty all Chinese men were required as a token of their submission to the Manchus to have the front of the head shaved and the rest of the hair uncut and worn in a plaited queue down the back. With the revolution of 1911 this practice disappeared but many men had the entire head shaved regularly, a fashion which suited them very well. European men with shaven heads look like criminals but Chinese men in the same state appear neat and indeed benign.

Water was brought to the houses on creaking, single-wheeled barrows. Sanitation was also by barrow, one of the less attractive features of town life in the old China. It was, nevertheless, an efficient system and no human waste was wasted. In the growing months it was used as fertilizer by market gardeners around the city, and in winter it was dried for future use. The system produced fine vegetables and less disease than might have been expected because of the high temperatures at which Chinese food is cooked. Similarly, although there were occasional outbreaks of cholera in summer there was relatively little water-borne disease because water was nearly always consumed in the form of tea made with boiled water.

Rickshaws were everywhere, powered by men who aged rapidly with the hard work, especially during the bitter winter months. A cry of '*Yang-ch'e*' (foreign cart) would generally bring several rickshaws running to bargain with the potential passenger. This harsh side of life in Peking between the two world wars has been vividly portrayed in Lao She's famous novel, *Rickshaw*. Human labour was also in general use to power other kinds of short distance transport. As the years passed many of the old-fashioned two-wheeled rickshaws were replaced by more efficient and less stable three-wheeled bicycle rickshaws, but almost all degrading human labour of this kind has been abolished since the revolution of 1949.

Hawkers were supplemented by stall-holders who set up little stalls or displayed their wares on the roadsides along important thoroughfares. All kinds of second-hand articles might be found in such stalls, as well as cheap manufactured goods. Stall-holders congregated in particular at the four regular markets in different quarters of the city. The markets were held in and around disused temples on certain days of every month and the stall-holders followed the progression from one locality to another. At these markets all kinds of goods were available for sale. The patent medicine sellers were particularly conspicuous, relying on their sales patter, the beating of gongs and the performance of feats of strength or agility to attract a crowd of onlookers from whom a few buyers would generally emerge.

For sale also were pets, including many cage birds trapped largely on the spring and autumn migrations, though some of the most valuable were imported from other parts of China. The Chinese were great bird fanciers, their techniques quite different from those of Western aviculturists. In the West the bird is provided with the maximum amount of space, whereas in China birds were kept in small, ornamental cages which could easily be carried from place to place by the bird's owner, the cage contained in a neatly fitting cover. The finest songbirds, the *pai-ling* (Mongolian Lark) and the *hua-mei* (Spectacled Laughing Thrush), could be so carried and taken to tea houses where bird fanciers would congregate and songs would be compared.

Nervous birds such as Ruby-throats and Blue-throats would be forcibly tamed by a unique Chinese system. The bird, with its tail and wing feathers neatly tied to prevent fraying, would be tethered by the neck to a perch. At first it would continually jump off and be left suspended by the neck. The bird man would patiently replace it on its perch until the bird came to realize, quite quickly, that life would be easier if it kept still. Eventually it would lose its fear and could be accommodated in a small round cage without dashing itself against the bars.

Certain grosbeaks could be taught to fly up and retrieve small balls flung high into the air. Crossbills were used by fortune-tellers: the bird would fly to a box, open it and select a card from which the future could be foretold. Falconry was still practised in the countryside and hooded hawks, generally goshawks, could be bought in the market.

Another form of recreation that I associate with the markets was kite flying. This was carried out at the time of the New Year, when market stalls would abound with kites. Peking people were expert kite flyers. Kites made of bamboo and paper existed in an extraordinary variety of designs and sizes: birds, goldfish, mythical characters and animals. Some were simple to fly, others much more complicated.

Stalls and markets were only two forms of retailing. There were also large permanent shops engaged in particular trades. Some trades were grouped together but others, such as grain shops, were well distributed throughout the city. Shops were elaborately publicized by sign-boards giving the name of the firm and the nature of the wares for sale. The fact that Chinese characters were traditionally written in columns made possible intensive sign-boarding in narrow streets. Many fine old traditional sign-boards which would nowadays be rated as works of art were to be seen, and many old established shops had finely carved exteriors. These shops were generally family businesses with many family members as shop assistants.

Midway between the shops and stalls were certain permanent markets which catered for every kind of business. The best-known of these was Tung An Shih Ch'ang (the Eastern Peace Market) at the northern end of Wang Fu Ching Ta Chieh in the East City. This was a two-storey warren of shops, stalls, restaurants and other places of entertainment, which was open all day but which was most lively at night. Everything from second-hand European books to cameras, radios, antiques and fresh fruit could be bought, and some of the best restaurants in Peking were located here.

After the Japanese established control in 1937 opium dens were openly allowed in Tung An Shih Ch'ang as well as in many other places in Peking. There was one opium den to which I was first taken by a German friend that I came to know well and where I took many photographs. Opium smoking was not uncommon among European bachelors though I never heard of a case of serious addiction. The den I visited might originally have been a shop house. It was situated on the corner of a small intersection in the East City, opposite a police station. Inside the entrance of the den was a curtain giving access to a long windowless room lined on each side with benches on which the smokers lay. Attendants brought them opium and the necessary implements: a pipe, an oil lamp and what looked like a long hatpin. A little ball of opium was put on the end of the pin, heated over the lamp, placed in the narrow pipe bowl and inhaled. It was a friendly, club-like place where customers dropped in at any time of the day or night. Some customers were heavy smokers but most would drop in for a pipe or two and then depart to carry on with their normal business.

The smoking of opium was not a Chinese invention. Although the medicinal qualities of opium had been known in China for centuries, the practice of smoking it came in with tobacco from The Philippines and Java. The two were originally smoked as a mixture, but the habit grew and the smoking of pure opium was a later Chinese refinement.

The streets were the scene of colourful wedding and funeral processions. Every Chinese family, rich and poor alike, sought to honour these occasions to the utmost limit permitted by their family resources. Indeed many families seriously impoverished themselves as a result even though it was the custom for friends and guests to give presents which included financial contributions towards the expenses. The ceremonies themselves were elaborate. They were held largely in the home, but processions were an essential element conducted with ceremony through the streets and accompanied by music. The organization was in the hands of specialist firms which hired out the paraphernalia and provided the necessary staff. The latter wore green gowns ornamented with stencilled designs, and conical hats of the same shape as those used by Manchu dynasty officials, topped with red tassels.

In the case of a funeral the coffin, often bought years before, would be brought to the house of the deceased and sometimes taken right into the house. This was made easier by the fact that the weight of a traditional Peking house was borne by wooden posts and so walls and windows could readily be knocked out and replaced later. After the body had lain in state for the prescribed period the coffin would be taken for burial on a catafalque, the size of which depended on the means of the deceased's family. It would be accompanied by musicians and the chief mourners, garbed in white, and often by priests of various persuasions. Also garbed in white would be various professional assistants who would carry paper models of things likely to be needed in the next world, such as houses, horses and carts. These models would be burned as it was believed that they would be miraculously recreated in solid or live form in the hereafter. Paper money was also burned or thrown into the air during the procession.

In the case of marriages the processions were made up of sedan chairs and their escorts and accompanying musicians. These would be sent to collect the bride and bring her to the bridegroom's house. The sedan chairs were substantial, curtained, box-like structures with curved roofs, red tassels hanging from the corners and topped by pewter balls. Propriety demanded three sedan chairs: one for the bride and two for matrons of honour who played an essential role in fetching and escorting the bride.

The chair-bearers, musicians and other attendants carrying ceremonial objects such as flags and imitation swords and spears would assemble at the house of the bridegroom. From here they would set out for the bride's house accompanied by certain male guests and led by two attendants with flags emblazoned with the characters reading 'Clear the way'.

There were thus two processions, one in each direction, as well as much exchange of presents, ritual feasting and other ceremonies. For a wealthy family the ceremonial was very complex and costly. By the thirties the old customs were beginning to give way to simpler and more economical procedures, celebrated largely at restaurants, but old-style processions were still common in Peking. Detailed accounts of a funeral and of a wedding in a wealthy Chinese family are to be found in H.Y. Lowe's splendid book, *The Adventures of Wu*.

Fortune-tellers roamed the streets and set up their booths on the pavements. There was much belief in astrology and divination, and fortune-telling was a learned profession much followed by blind men who might be seen in the streets armed with a blind man's staff in one hand and a clapper in the other. There were various systems of fortune-telling but in most the fortune-teller needed to know the year, month, day and hour of birth of his client. These details would provide eight characters and from the relationship between them the fortune-teller would deduce his client's future. In a common form of footpath divination the enquirer shook out from a bamboo container a sliver of bamboo on which were written certain characters relating to the planets and constellations. These would be looked up in the fortune-teller's essential handbook, an official almanac, part astronomical and part astrological, and dating back to Ming times.

There was no lack of beggars in the streets but they were well distributed and had their own beats. One became familiar with certain beggars who frequented particular areas and temple festivals always had their quota. It was a profession of a kind, its most unpleasant side being the deliberate exploitation of gaping sores and ulcers to arouse the horror and revulsion of members of the public, forcing them to give a quick donation so as to be rid of the beggar.

I had so little money that I was in no danger of being tempted to buy things but I often had to take friends of Miss Bieber shopping and came to know many of the specialist traders. In the early mornings there was the Jade Market outside Ha Ta Men. Foreigners referred to this as the Thieves' Market but this was unjustified. It was more like a miniature antique dealers' fair, where representatives of dealers from all over the city would congregate to trade with each other and with other customers who were early risers. Most of the objects for sale were small and easily transported, and the turnover was rapid. You never knew what you might see there and you could be quite sure that you would be unlikely to see it again.

In the Chinese City there was one street which specialized in second-hand furniture, a mecca for the few foreigners who were interested in classical Chinese furniture. This furniture is quite different from the ornate, heavily carved furniture from south China which has generally been exported to the West. Chinese furniture of the seventeenth and eighteenth centuries and earlier had beautiful proportions and an almost austere simplicity. It was made from a very few kinds of fine cabinet woods. The workmanship and intricate joinery were unique, the dealers a most patient breed. Their shops were so full of furniture that to examine a piece at the back of the shop it was often necessary to move all the rest of the contents to obtain a clear view. And this did not always lead to a sale.

Especially fascinating were the premises dealing in antique Chinese carpets from west China and Sinkiang. Although not of such fine weave as Persian carpets, these Chinese carpets had great charm. Some came on the market from private owners in Peking and from temples but many of those for sale were still reaching Peking from west China and Sinkiang, a trade that continued to some extent even after the Japanese invasion of 1937. The principal carpet merchants, Mr Sammy Lee and Mr David Wang, had a wonderful stock in their premises outside Ch'ien Men. There were carpets with dull red backgrounds from Kansu, and blue-and-gold and blue-and-white carpets from Ninghsia, all decorated with typically Chinese and often Buddhist designs. From Sinkiang came rugs showing Central Asian and Muslim influence. After the outbreak of the Pacific War when business was slack, I sometimes called at the carpet merchants to be shown their treasures. Also available were many modern carpets, made mainly in Tientsin, and some in Peking itself, but these lacked the gentle colours and the elegance of design of the traditional carpets.

Boy in a Mongol hat. This was a common and very necessary form of headwear
in the bitter cold of the north China winter.

The passing scene receiving the attention of a group of children.

Family group taking the winter sunshine.

Itinerant toy-seller discussing business with a young customer.

The reed toy-maker, who would make his appearance in the summer
and weave fresh reeds into a variety of wonderful shapes while you watched.

Paper collector. Collecting paper and rags was one of the poorest occupations.
Nothing that could possibly be reused or recycled was ever wasted, and
the paper collectors supplied the raw material for recycling into coarse paper.

Beggar woman and her child. Over the years I often
saw her and she was nearly always pregnant.

The coffin shop. An old man sits in the shelter of a pile
of cedar planks in the warmth of the winter sun. Coffins would often be bought years
before a person's death and while he was still in the best of health.

Seamstresses sewing characters on to cloth banners. They were taking advantage
of the winter sun and a windless day. Chinese houses were very cold
in winter and the warmth of the sun was always welcome.

The northern end of Ch'ien Men Street after snow had fallen and quickly begun to melt.

Terrible dust storms occurred in the Peking winter. In the distance
is the Fox Tower at the south-eastern corner of the Tartar City.

Rickshaws provided cheap and efficient transport but at the expense of human lives.

Sleeping rickshaw man.

The woman with the child had been bargaining with the rickshaw men in the foreground.
As part of the bargaining process she turns to walk away but will be
called back by the man who accepts the fare offered. It was arduous work
for the pullers who suffered especially during the bitterly harsh north China winter.

An old-fashioned shop front adorned with finely carved woodwork and elegant lattice windows.
Only the centre pane was glass; the remainder was made of paper.

One of the streets in the Chinese City, south-east of Ch'ien Men.
Long-gowned citizens padded quietly about their business in their cloth-soled shoes.

The sign of the opium smoker — the gesture told its own story.

The old lady who ran the opium den that I visited.
She was not averse to a pipe herself when business was slack.

Opium smoker and his son. A derelict actor, he died not long afterwards
and the people of the opium den cared for the little boy.

Wedding procession, probably on its way to pick up the bride. Old-style weddings
were cheerful, colourful affairs accompanied by much trumpet-blowing. Weddings and funerals
were expensive and it was a point of honour for a family to spend as
much as they could afford — and often more — on such ceremonies.

One of the trumpeters
of a wedding procession.

A young wedding attendant
stretching out his hand for a donation.

Funeral procession. The richer the family, the bigger was the catafalque to convey
the elaborate coffin which had often been bought years before by the deceased.
The procession would pause periodically to enable those taking part
to catch up and to give the catafalque-bearers a rest.

White was the colour of mourning, worn both by members of the family
and by funeral functionaries here throwing paper money into the air to appease the spirits.
Paper money was also burned as it was believed that in the hereafter
it would be miraculously converted into real currency.

Priests, in this case Buddhists, would accompany the funeral procession
to provide music and to chant Buddhist sutras.

Principal mourners pause to make obeisance to the coffin.

Roadside fortune-teller. Peking people never tired of having their fortunes told and such forecasts
were often an important guide to current action. From the container in the foreground
the client would shake out a sliver of bamboo, on which were inscribed certain characters.
From a study of these and reference to booklets arranged around the centre-piece,
decorated with the Eight Trigrams that provide the symbolic foundation for divination,
the fortune-teller would advise his client as to what the future held for him.

Many fortune-tellers were blind and roamed the streets
beating a small hand-gong to advertise their presence.

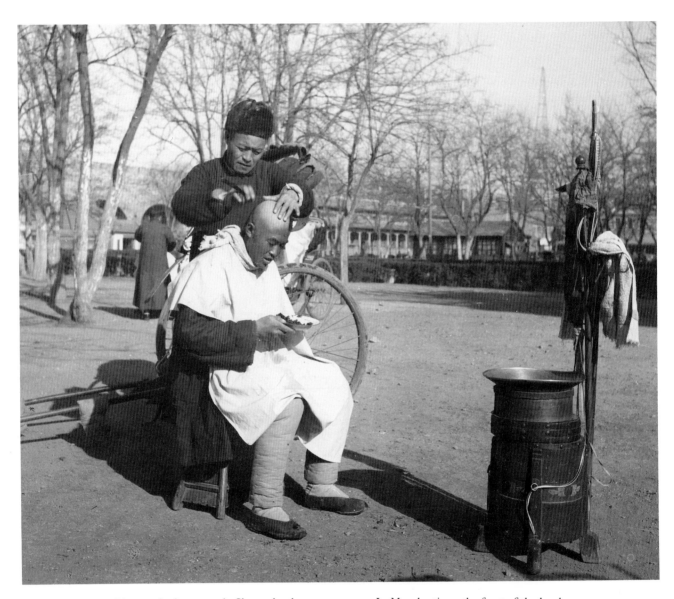

Itinerant barber at work. Shaven heads were common. In Manchu times the front of the head
was shaved and the hair on the back of the head was grown into a queue. When queues disappeared after the
revolution of 1911, men found it comfortable and convenient to have the whole head shaved.

A seller of sewing thread advertising his wares with a hand-drum.

T'ien Ch'iao market was a permanent outdoor market to the west of
Ch'ien Men Street and not far from the Altar of Heaven. Here could
be bought all kinds of second-hand goods for the home.

Feather duster seller. Peking was a dry and dusty place
and feather dusters were always in demand.

A man who made ornamental sweets from coloured rice flour.

The sweet-maker made a variety of little figures
and objects, the most elaborate being tiny human puppets.

A sweet-maker who blew molten toffee
into a wonderful variety of shapes.

At Lung Fu Ssu many cage birds were sold during the spring and autumn migrations.

Lady customer at Lung Fu Ssu market.

The bird fancier. The light, ornamental cage would have been enclosed in
a cloth cover and carried by the fancier on his stroll until he sat down
to smoke his pipe and let his pet Ruby-throat enjoy the sunlight.

Close-up of a tethered Ruby-throat, its tail and wing feathers neatly tied to prevent
fluttering and fraying. The Siberian Ruby-throat was one of the most popular species.
They were initially tethered to little stands and forcibly tamed.

A gentleman of the old school looks over a stall in Liu Li Ch'ang.

The New Year Fair at Liu Li Ch'ang was of special importance
for the sale of paintings and other works of art.

Jujube seller. Jujubes, which bear a close resemblance to dates, are the fruit
of a thorny tree that grows in north China. The fruit is pitted
and dried for consumption during the winter months.

Crab-apples, another popular fruit, candied and impaled on wooden skewers.

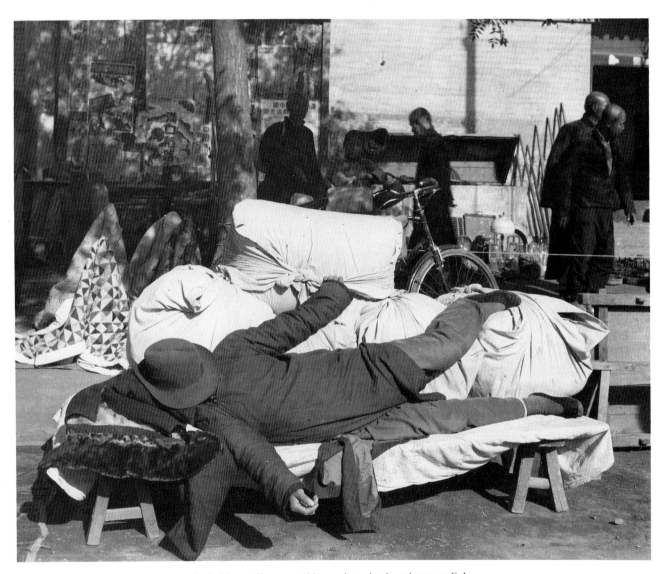

A clothing stall-owner taking a siesta in the winter sunlight.

Selling bed quilts and heavy overcoats at the onset of winter. Winter clothing, made mainly of cotton and heavily wadded with raw cotton, was warm, light, comfortable and cheap.

A Peking grain shop, the various goods neatly displayed and priced.

Food and Entertainment

As the heart of a once great and sophisticated civilization, Peking retained a tradition of fine cooking. Every kind of regional cooking was to be found there and there was a variety of cooking to suit every taste. Many of the restaurants were ancient establishments which had been in operation since the heyday of imperial China. The large restaurants were, of course, for the rich, but hawkers and street kitchens also provided extraordinarily appetizing food. The skills of the cooks were unsurpassed.

If I had to nominate a favourite kind of food it would be a simple food which anyone who could afford to eat could afford to buy. This was the *shao-ping*, a flat, round bun made from coarse wholemeal flour, with a somewhat pastry-like consistency and a topping of sesame seeds. It was a most tasty form of bread even when eaten by itself but it could also be stuffed with meats and was a delicious ingredient for a European breakfast. Like so many good things it was too common to be fully appreciated.

As north China is predominantly a wheat-growing area there were many kinds of wheat noodles. In a noodle shop you could watch the noodles themselves being made from dough that was kneaded and rolled, the cook interspersing the rolling with loud tattoos beaten with the rolling-pin. The noodle maker seemed able to impart some magical elasticity to the dough, and when he pulled out a long roll of dough between his hands and flicked it downwards the dough would behave as if it was made of rubber. You could have boiled noodles or fried noodles, generally topped with some tasty meat and vegetables. A good bowl of Peking noodles was a meal in itself.

Allied to noodles were various kinds of meat dumplings made with extraordinary dexterity. The dumpling maker would pick up a small pancake-shaped piece of dough in one hand, place a little meat filling in it with the other hand and then close the ends of the pancake around the filling and put the neatly wrapped little parcel aside before starting on the next one. The whole operation was done with great speed, the dumplings themselves marvellously identical in size and appearance. There were round dumplings (*pao-tzu*) and kidney-shaped dumplings (*chiao-tzu*) both of which were steamed. Fried *chiao-tzu* were called *kuo-t'ieh*. The contents were usually minced pork, vegetables and ginger.

Shao-ping were not the only form of bread. The other main variety was steamed bread (*man-t'ou*). This lacked the gourmet quality of the *shao-ping* but was a good and solid form of bread and very hygienic. Not only was it steamed but in the process it formed a skin on the outside which could readily be peeled off. There were many kinds and shapes of *man-t'ou*, some of which had nutritious stuffings of ground beans or pork.

I was not expert in the enormous range of fine dishes that were available in Peking. I ate elaborate food only when invited. The majority of the restaurants were run by Shantung people but there were many other provincial styles available. I especially remember the Szechuan restaurants which had unusually hot and spicy food. Quite a number of the best restaurants were Muslim which demonstrated that fine Chinese cooking is not wholly dependent on the pig. Nevertheless pork is a fundamental ingredient in most forms of Chinese cooking and there was one ancient institution in the West City, the Sha Kuo Chü, which served nothing else. A way had been found to cook every part of the animal and it was all delicious. If I remember rightly the smallest number of dishes that could be ordered was eight, and there was a range of thirty-two or more.

There was a wonderful atmosphere of conviviality and cheerful uproar in a good Peking restaurant operating at full steam. Service was extraordinarily quick except at party banquets which were purposely long drawn out to allow time for plenty of conversation. At any ordinary meal freshly cooked dishes appeared as if by magic. If you wanted the waiter you cried '*Wei*' and it seemed as if all the waiters gave voice to an answering '*Wei*' before your own waiter came bustling in to serve your needs. There was plenty of good yellow rice wine (Shao Hsing) which tastes a little like sherry and was imported from the place of the same name in east China. It is consumed hot in little cups and with many toasts. By a polite convention a lady could be toasted but was not obliged to empty her own cup. She could nominate one of the gentlemen present to act as her representative and empty a cup on her behalf. The more plebeian drink was rough, raw spirit (*pai-kan*) made from sorghum.

There was often far too much to eat at a restaurant meal and it was quite acceptable to take the leftovers home wrapped up in neat little parcels. Another convention required the guest of honour to face the door and the host to have his back to it so that any assassin would be more likely to stab the host and not the guest. There were various party games in which the loser had to drink a cup of wine. The most common was the fist game in which two players would simultaneously extend one to five fingers from their closed fist, or keep the fist closed and attempt to guess the total number of fingers extended. It could be a very uproarious game.

Very popular among foreigners were the duck restaurants. The Peking ducks were large white birds. Those destined for the table had short lives as they were forcibly crammed with food from an early age and were best eaten when they were between ten and twelve weeks old. They were very fat and very tender, and were cooked in large brick ovens until the skin was brown, shiny and crisp. The duck would then be produced as the main item of a meal which could include duck livers, tongues, feet and duck soup. The bird would be finely sliced and the slices — a little skin (the most important part), a little fat and a little meat — would be daubed with sweet bean sauce and eaten wrapped up in a small pancake with the addition of spring onions. The last thing to be brought to the table was the head, neatly sliced open, so that the guest of honour could eat the brains.

It seems that duck restaurants were a relatively late innovation. Originally various bake-houses roasted chickens and ducks as a form of take-away food for home consumption as few private homes had the large ovens needed for perfect roasting. Bake-houses still existed and you could buy roast ducks and chickens neatly wrapped up for home use or as presents. So-called Peking duck is now commonly available in Chinese restaurants all over the world but the way it is served is not as refined as it was in Peking.

Although not strictly speaking Chinese, certain popular Muslim restaurants served excellent mutton dishes. They were known as Mongolian dishes but more probably originated in Central Asia. One of these styles involved cooking finely sliced mutton in a charcoal chafing dish. The meat cooked very quickly and was then dipped into a bowl of sauce which each diner had mixed to suit his own taste from various ingredients brought to the table. The dipping not only cooled off the meat but also gave it a fine flavour and it was eaten with *shao-ping*. Cabbage, small onions and vermicelli were also cooked in the chafing dish, and pickled leeks were served as a side dish. The meat could be augmented with slices of fat taken from the tails of the peculiar fat-tailed sheep of Asia which develop large, bulbous tails that are almost entirely fat.

In the other form of Mongolian cooking, meat and a few vegetables were soused in a mixture of soy sauce and vinegar, then grilled and stuffed into large *shao-ping*. The accompaniment to these dishes should properly be fiery *pai-kan*. They were both splendid forms of meal on a cold winter's night.

At some restaurants beef rather than mutton was grilled. I well remember one such establishment in the Chinese City called Niu Jou Wan which was presided over by a tall and dignified old Muslim. The beef was grilled in an open courtyard and no bills were produced. When the meal was finished the proprietor announced the bill — so many plates of beef, so many *shao-ping*, so many catties of wine — and in this way all those present in the restaurant could take pleasure from the knowledge that you had eaten well. And when you paid, the amount of the tip was also announced.

For Buddhists there were fine vegetarian restaurants in which many of the dishes were artfully contrived to resemble meat dishes in appearance but which were entirely devoid of any animal content. There were dishes in the forms of roast duck or baked fish, and in many other guises, the basic ingredient of which was bean flour. Together with the vegetable dishes they had all the richness and variety of flavours derived from spices and sauces that characterize good Chinese cooking.

As befits a civilized people who have been familiar with alcohol for thousands of years, the Chinese are moderate and sensible drinkers. Although throughout their history certain Chinese have been addicted to the bottle and although there could be hearty convivial drinking at dinner parties, drunkenness was no problem in Chinese society. Heavy drinking was rare. I do not recollect having ever seen a drunk Chinese in the streets of Peking.

Entertainment was by no means confined to eating. There was unending and rich entertainment freely available to all in the streets, markets and temples. Each season brought its own spectacles and activities. There were always staged entertainments to be seen.

South of Ch'ien Men, adjoining what had been a fine marble bridge, T'ien Ch'iao (the Bridge of Heaven), over a canal on the way to the Altar of Heaven, there was a large permanent market where many kinds of goods were for sale. Various forms of entertainment were also to be seen here at times of festival. There were wonderful acrobats and jugglers, many of them quite young children. There were stilt dancers, story-tellers and travelling theatrical troupes who performed under makeshift mat sheds. The performers were not permanently in Peking but toured the towns and villages of north China as well. The travelling theatre provided entertainment for those who could not afford to visit the permanent theatres.

There were a number of theatres which throughout the year performed plays and operas drawn from China's great heritage of drama that had evolved during centuries of interest in the theatre. The plays conformed to the structure of Western theatre and were divided into acts and scenes in the same way but stage techniques were radically different. The old Chinese theatre was almost bare of scenery, there was no curtain, and the seats were simple wooden benches. The stage hands wandered about openly and the orchestra sat on the sides of the stage in full view of the public. Performances went on until late in the night, the main and best act being the final one. The actors wore splendid traditional costumes and make-up but the scenery and stage props and much of the action were merely indicated by a large number of well understood conventions.

For example, two tables covered with red cloth, one on top of each other and surmounted by a chair, represented a throne or judgment seat; two bamboo poles with cloth attached, a city wall or gate; two yellow flags with a wheel drawn on each, a chariot. Trumpets off-stage heralded the approach of cavalry; fireworks, the appearance of a demon.

Make-up and costumes indicated various types of character. A red face meant a sacred or loyal person or a great emperor. An honest but uncouth fellow had a black face; a villain, a white patch on the nose. A white face betokened cunning and treachery. Devils had green faces, deities yellow faces. An emperor wore yellow embroidered with dragons winding up and down; high officials wore yellow with dragons flying downwards. A courtesan wore jewellery and gaudy clothes, a virtuous woman, plain black with blue sleeve trimmings.

Lifting a foot high up indicated that the actor was stepping over a threshhold; bringing the hands together slowly closed the door; a whip held in the right hand meant that the actor was mounting a horse, a whip held in the left hand that he was dismounting. Standing rigidly behind a pillar suggested that a person was in hiding; slowly moving the hands across the face that he was weeping. There were many more conventions and all were well understood by the Chinese theatre-goer.

The parts were both spoken and sung and the comparative lack of movement on stage was compensated for by weapon play and acrobatics performed by subsidiary actors. The atmosphere was remarkably informal despite the formality of the performance itself. Performances went on for hours, consisting generally not of one long play but of a whole succession of short plays or sections of longer ones. The audience came and went, gossiped and drank tea. Whole families would come to the theatre. Attendants served tea and other refreshments and hot towels. The latter would often be hurled with unerring accuracy from one attendant to another as this was quicker than carrying them through the audience. But although there was continual noise from the audience its members nevertheless did not let their attention stray too far from the stage. A finely rendered song or spectacular acrobatics would still be greeted with cries of acclamation from the audience, nearly all of whom would be familiar with the play being performed.

All the performers were men, the female impersonators speaking and singing in falsetto voices. The stage had not always been confined to actors, however. The prohibition on women dated back to an edict by the Emperor Ch'ien Lung whose mother had been an actress. Although acting had become a respected profession, this had not always been the case: in imperial times an actor's descendants were forbidden to sit for the imperial civil service examinations for three generations.

Roasting Peking duck in the large brick oven which ensured the most thorough and uniform roasting. This was done at the entrance to the restaurant.

Baking *ma-ping*, a kind of small bun.

A common breakfast snack in the streets of Peking consisted of
lengths of batter fried in oil, here prepared by that rare
phenomenon, a left-handed person.

Steamed bread, *man-t'ou*, was cooked on bamboo slats set in circular bamboo containers.

A bowl of soup eaten (again by a left-handed person) with excellent
sesame-covered *shao-ping* buns, three of which are in the foreground of the photograph.
The *shao-ping* is one of the best, and commonest, culinary creations of Peking.

The proprietor of Niu Jou Wan, a grilled beef restaurant. In his hostelry
there were no written accounts. The details of the bill and the amount
of the tip were announced by the proprietor in a stentorian voice.

Chinese cooks have a remarkable ability to cut
wafer-thin slices of meat with large cleavers.

Meat and vegetables were marinated in vinegar and soy
sauce, quickly cooked on the grill and eaten stuffed
into a large version of the *shao-ping*.

Refreshment seller purveying a rather bitter plum juice drink
and the hand clappers with which he announced his presence.

Itinerant refreshment stall for children. Wherever there might be a demand, there would be some specialist hawker filling the needs of even the smallest customer.

Itinerant food-seller, his panniers ornamented with well polished brass.

A wayside seller of strong liquor. The little pewter bottles contain
the strong raw *pai-kan* of north China made from sorghum grain.

A Chinese theatre in Peking in the thirties was a study in contrast:
between the formality of beautiful costumes and stylized movement and diction, and the informality
of stage-hands in full view, musicians in the wings, and hats and teacups on the front
of the stage. Members of the audience chatted cheerfully among themselves.

Young actors in a Peking garden. It was still customary for men
to impersonate female characters. Mastering the falsetto voices of the
female characters called for much training and practice.

Actor portraying an emperor. His face was painted red and he wore an elaborate gown.

An actor in the role of Sun Wu K'ung, the monkey who, according to tradition,
helped to procure sacred Buddhist sutras from the west.

A man with performing mice which would climb the ladders and make their way
through the rings of the frame while the puppet master gave an accompaniment. The mice,
probably some kind of hamster, were a never-failing source of interest to children.

Itinerant puppet show. The puppet master would roam the streets and set up his booth on the street or in a private courtyard, whenever it was wanted.

Puppet, actuated by hand from below.

Nowadays Chinese acrobatics and juggling are world-famous but they are descended
from an ancient form of popular entertainment which was always to be seen
at T'ien Ch'iao during holidays and festivals. Children started to train
in these skills almost as soon as they could walk.

Patent medicine sellers were much in evidence at fairs. This man was selling
body-building unguents. Stripped to the waist in the north China mid-winter, he was
flexing a powerful bow and so demonstrating the excellence of his jaws and teeth.

Schoolboys under martial arts instruction. Traditional martial arts skills and acrobatics
were preserved in the theatre and for popular entertainment.

In the early morning elderly gentlemen practised *t'ai-chi*,
the ancient Chinese system of exercises designed to perfect body balance.

Kite flying was a popular pastime at all levels of society,
and splendid kites were sold in the spring.

Another popular pastime was skating. This veteran skater used to perform on Pei Hai,
and in his younger days had performed for the Empress Dowager.

A quiet game of chess in a rich man's home. The game is a contest between two armies separated by a river. As in Western chess there are sixteen pieces on each side though their designations and moves are different. The chessmen are simple counters inscribed with the function of the individual piece.

Arts and Crafts

CRAFT work in all its diversity was something that never ceased to fascinate me. The tradition of fine craftsmanship, derived from Peking's long history as a great imperial capital, was still strong, and many of the techniques were much as they had been for centuries. Some of the techniques and tools were strange to a Westerner, but the skills of the workers were unsurpassed. Even the simplest task such as wrapping up a parcel was marked by distinctive neatness and elegance.

Craft work was often localized in certain areas of the city. Many of the producing units were organized in guilds designed for protection and the settlement of disputes. Boys started their apprenticeship at an early age and, since the workers generally remained specialists in their calling throughout their lives, it was hardly surprising that they achieved such high levels of skill. The hours of work were extremely long and holidays almost non-existent except at the New Year. But nothing was more impressive than the cheerfulness and good humour of the craftsmen. The work units were small. The bosses worked as hard as the workers and generally they ate their midday meal together. One never had the impression of oppressive, sweated labour.

There was such a profusion of crafts that it is difficult to classify them neatly. They fell into two main categories. On the one hand there were utilitarian craftsmen such as carpenters, builders, stonemasons, metalworkers and others producing goods for everyday use. On the other hand there were the craftsmen whose work was related to the arts: stone carvers, silversmiths, scroll mounters and many more. But there was considerable overlap. The stonemason could adorn his work with elegant carvings or ornamentation and the window maker could produce the lattice work to be papered over in designs of traditional good taste. The characteristic that the workers shared was a capacity for fine workmanship and a part-instinctive and part-traditional feeling for good design.

There were whole streets and neighbourhoods dedicated to one particular calling. To the west of the road running south through the Chinese City from the great central gateway of Ch'ien Men there were many craft communities. One of the first on this street, Ch'ien Men Street, was Jade Street, which was lined with shops selling jades and other stone carvings. Here the sales and business deals took place, and nearby, often behind the shops, were the work places where craftsmen produced the goods.

Jade was of special importance in old China. For the Chinese it was the most valued of precious stones and imbued with many magical and curative properties. The term jade referred to two different stones: nephrite, which occurred in various colours including white, dull yellow, brown and green; and jadeite, the brilliant green stone usually used for jewellery in this century. Jade is found in many parts of the world but most of the jades of old China came from Turkistan.

Jade was used for many ceremonial and religious purposes. Not only was it appreciated for its beauty but also for the cool, almost sensuous feeling that it conveyed when handled and for the sonorous notes emitted by jade chimes. Such chimes of L-shaped stones of various sizes suspended from stands were played as an important part of Confucian rites.

In the thirties the carving of jade was mainly for jewellery and ornaments, many of which were exported. Some of the finest jewellery, especially green jades, were reworked pieces derived from the heirlooms of impoverished gentry. It is sometimes difficult to distinguish the finest modern carving from work done in earlier times.

Jade Street led into Liu Li Ch'ang which specialized in books and paintings. In workshops books were still printed on woodblocks and bound in the traditional manner. Here too were specialists in the mounting and restoration of paintings.

The art of painting developed early in China and followed principles of space depiction and perspective that were different from those in the West. It was closely related to poetry and calligraphy. Paintings were not intended for permanent display, being mounted on scrolls to be kept securely in chests. Fine paintings would only be hung or shown when the need arose. A great collection of Chinese paintings could be housed in a fraction of the space required for the same number of Western paintings.

New paintings had to be mounted and old ones needed to be repaired or restored. This was work of exquisite skill carried out on long, highly polished, dark red lacquer tables in the same way as it had been for centuries past.

North and south of Jade Street were similar streets specializing in lanterns, jewellery and silks. On the other side of Ch'ien Men Street were brass and pewter workers, silversmiths, embroiderers and furriers.

In the shops and markets where contemporary craft work and all the other objects that had come down from an enormously rich and cultured heritage were to be found for sale, as well as in most other shops and markets selling both new and second-hand goods, bargaining was the almost invariable practice. The price initially quoted was rarely the price that the seller expected to receive. The final price was decided upon by a polite process of negotiation and discussion. Sometimes agreement could not be reached, in which case negotiations ended without any hard feelings on either side so long as the price offered bore a reasonable relationship to the true value of the object being bargained for. A successful session of bargaining should leave both buyer and seller contented.

It was not a hurried process. The buyer would put forward the case for a lower price and draw attention to any perceived imperfections in the object of the bargaining. The seller would stress its good points. The buyer might regretfully withdraw, and then have second thoughts. The seller would probably try to accommodate the second thoughts to some extent. And so it went on until a mutually satisfactory compromise was reached. The better the humour, the more likely was the seller to relent, and if the seller could be induced to smile, the buyer was doing well. Brusqueness or impatience on the part of the buyer would certainly not bring the price down. In the markets dealers could still be seen dickering over a price by a confidential system which left the onlooker with no clue as to the nature of the negotiations. They would clasp their hands concealed by the ends of their long sleeves and convey their offers and counter offers by a system of hand signals. In this way commercial confidentiality was preserved.

Not all craftsmen worked indoors. Some simple goods were made on the footpath while you waited, especially some kinds of sweets and children's toys. Toffee was blown into intricate shapes by a process akin to glass blowing. It was not an entirely hygienic process but produced artistic results. Another kind of toffee was poured freehand into lattice designs. Simple toys, such as frogs or fish, were made from coloured rice flour or, in the summer, woven from freshly cut reeds. Some textile processes requiring ample space, such as forming silk floss into thread, were also performed out-of-doors.

Some of the heavier goods were made outside Peking. Tile and brick kilns were located near the coal-mines of Men T'ou Kou in the nearer Western Hills. Tiles and bricks for general household use were a uniform grey in colour but the kilns also produced the brightly coloured golden, green and blue tiles and mythical rooftop animals for ornamental buildings and for the restoration and repair of imperial temples and palaces. In the same district were foundries producing iron bowls and cooking pots. Iron was also used for the making of ornamental tracery.

Rough paper was still being made by hand, the process little changed from that first invented in China in the first century. The only difference was that the raw material I saw was generally recycled paper and rags instead of rice straw and bamboo. The raw materials were ground up, mixed with water and reduced to a slurry. A worker would then dip out sheets of particles caught on a fine screen and the sheets would be pasted up on walls to dry.

Some particularly ancient crafts and the remnants of others were still to be seen. One of the most important of the former was the making of musical instruments. China has a rich and largely unique musical heritage. Apart from those of stone and some of the more elaborate instruments, one could still see many being made in Peking, especially the popular stringed and skin instruments. The more elaborate instruments existed for chamber music and for the recreation of the intelligentsia but music existed at every level of society. The main changes that have taken place in music involve the modernization of musical notation, not of the instruments themselves. Certain weapons, though no longer of practical use such as crossbows, were also still in production for recreational use.

Most of the craft work was undertaken by men, although women were employed in some of the fields that catered for the export trade such as the making of artificial flowers. Women did, however, play an important part in embroidery. Some of this was very elaborate, but simple embroidery was done especially to adorn children's clothing. Even the poorest mother would try to brighten her children's clothing with something colourful and attractive, usually patterns picked out in cross stitch. More elaborate stitches had been introduced for some work and for the export trade but examples of cross stitch and appliqué work were to be seen in even the most remote villages.

For ornamental themes the craft workers drew on the great wealth of Chinese symbolism derived from philosophy, religion and myth. From philosophy came such symbols as Yang and Yin, a circle divided into two interlocking parts and representing the active male principle Yang and the passive female principle Yin. Another philosophical concept was Pa Kua (the Eight Trigrams) representing in simple form — three superimposed lines in varying lengths and combinations — the elements which the Chinese believed made up the universe. From Buddhism came such symbols as the Endless Knot and the Buddha's Finger, a kind of citrus. Animals and birds, insects and plants, all made up a repertoire of designs and symbols to draw from in artistic and ornamental work.

To the craft workers whom I knew the symbols which they used repeatedly were little more than emblems of good luck. The traditional significance of the motifs had become obscured in the great cultural decline that had occurred in the previous hundred years. Even before that time much of the original significance of symbols had been modified by the impact of popular religion and superstition. A great deal, however, had been preserved in fine art and architecture. The Yang and Yin, the Yang red and the Yin black or colourless, represented the union of things spiritual and material. Around this symbol would often be grouped the Eight Trigrams. An outer circle might be added representing the signs of the zodiac, a concept derived from Central Asia. In the Chinese zodiac there were twelve animals, six of which were held to represent the Yang principle (dragon, tiger, horse, sheep, cock and snake) and six the Yin principle (rat, ox, hare, monkey, dog and pig).

Dragons have played an especially important role in symbolism. The heavenly dragon represented Yang and was an all important and beneficent animal for it brought the rains on which agriculture depended. It had become the symbol of China itself and the five-clawed dragon was reserved for the decorations of the emperor's personal possessions. A lesser four-clawed dragon was reserved for other members of the imperial family and, towards the end of imperial China, for high officials as well. Reserved for the empress was a splendid bird, called a phoenix by foreigners though it had none of the characteristics of the phoenix. Its portrayal seems to be based on the rare Ocellated Argus Pheasant of Indo-China.

Buddhism was the richest source of symbols. Outside most of the temples and palaces of Peking there were pairs of white marble Buddhist lions, the male playing with a ball and the female with a cub. They were to protect sacred buildings and to defend the law. Eight especially important Buddhist symbols were derived from India. The most important and the most commonly seen was the Lotus on which the Buddha sits enthroned. Its flower, leaf, seed-head and root section (which contains air chambers) were often portrayed in art objects. The remaining symbols of the eight were the Wheel of the Law, the Vase of the Water of Life, the Conch Shell (trumpet of victory), the Twin Fish (symbol of constancy), the Endless Knot (uninterrupted long life), and the Royal Canopy and the State Umbrella (symbols of temporal power).

Taoism also had its symbolism. From Taoism came the use of red (the colour of Yang) as the most auspicious colour. White and black (Yin) were avoided except that white was the colour used for funeral garments. Eight Taoist immortals, each identifiable by a particular attribute, were commonly represented. Medicinal plants were often portrayed, not on account of their beauty but because of their healing significance.

There were many other symbols founded on myth and tradition. The peach represented immortality, the peach tree longevity and marriage. Long life was also represented by the pine tree and by the *ling-chih* fungus. The pine, bamboo and early flowering plum blossom signified constancy because they maintain their colours during the dull days of winter. The lotus represented summer and the chrysanthemum autumn. The extensive use of symbols would constantly come to the attention of any observant visitor to China.

Not all Chinese crafts were to be seen in Peking. There were many regional specialities. For example, the main centres of porcelain production have always been in south and central China. I did, however, once come across a small workshop producing copies of T'ang figures and horses for the export market.

My work with Miss Bieber gave me some special familiarity with the making of jewellery which had always been a Peking speciality. Most of the jewellery was silver, which was the universal precious metal. Relatively little gold was used in China. Involvement with jewellery also required some knowledge of the various semi-precious stones and other materials that were used. Semi-precious stones were formerly of special importance in the making of Mandarin chains of office. There were pitfalls in acquiring some semi-precious stones because the Chinese had become adept at making very beautiful copies in glass. There was generally no dishonest intent in this practice; glassmakers were simply trying to reproduce some of the fine qualities of the stones. No reputable dealer would try to substitute one for the other.

Aquamarine, especially the more deeply coloured stones, was popular. Turquoise had been introduced from Central Asia and was popular under the Manchus. It varied in colour and sometimes the colour was improved with a little dye. The Chinese believed that green turquoise was the oldest kind. Turquoise requires special attention as its colour can be adversely affected by contact with perspiration and oily substances and even by exposure to strong sunlight. Lapis lazuli, malachite, carnelian and many forms of agate were also in frequent use. Rose quartz carvings were in constant demand for the export trade, although its beautiful colour is unstable if exposed to strong sunlight, as is that of amethyst.

Some Manchu jewellery had been made from kingfisher feathers though I think that the craft had died out long before I reached Peking. Other materials used in Chinese jewellery included amber, a very beautiful but very brittle substance, and red coral. Most of the stones came from west China and Central Asia, while red coral came from the South Seas.

A large proportion of the world's fine and decorative art has always been anonymous and nowhere was this more marked than in China. Although there were some exceptions it was only in painting and calligraphy that it was customary for the artist to sign his name. This is unlike the Japanese tradition where carvers, metalworkers and other craftsmen habitually signed their work. Even the men who created China's greatest bronzes and sculptures, and her most beautiful jade carvings and lacquer, were to remain unknown, mute testimony to a great artistic tradition.

Ch'i Pai Shih (1863-1957), the distinguished painter and calligrapher, at work in his studio. He specialized in painting flowers and aquatic life, especially crabs and prawns.

Ch'i Pai Shih and his young family.

Ch'i Pai Shih affixing his seal on a painting.

Wang Ch'ing Fang, another gifted artist. He painted landscapes in a style that was a break from tradition. Art was his vocation but he supported his family by teaching.

Painting was by no means an all male activity. There were many women artists.

The scroll mounters. Chinese paintings are executed on flimsy paper or silk
and must be mounted on protective pieces of silk. Fine paintings are
generally kept rolled up and are hung or, in the case of handscrolls,
unrolled only on special occasions or to show friends.

Repairing a painting prior to remounting, work calling for the most exacting skills.

The Chinese relative of the oboe.

A Chinese zither, one of the most valued of the great wealth of Chinese musical instruments.

A moon guitar.

A Chinese flute.

Writing the titles on a Chinese work of several volumes.

The bookshop. Old Chinese literary texts were frequently reprinted
with or without additional commentaries, resulting in an enormous literary output and
a great volume of work for booksellers, bibliophiles and librarians.

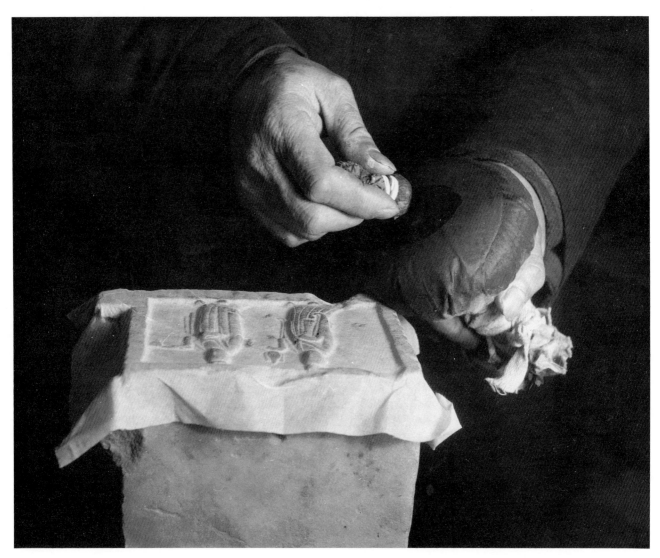

Making a rubbing.

A Peking businessman filling in a quiet moment by carving himself a seal.
All documents were signed by seals which are almost impossible to duplicate.
It was a very reliable system, so long as the seal did not fall into the wrong hands.

Mr Huang, the doyen of the dealers in antiquities, a very courteous
old gentleman with a great knowledge of Chinese art history.

Mr Huang and his staff.

Jade polisher at work.

Making artificial fruit, an ancient craft derived from glass-blowing
which had become largely an export business.

Carving lacquer. The lacquer consisted of many coats of resin mixed with a red colouring agent
and applied to wooden bases. When the coating was thick enough it was carved.

Cloisonné painting. Cloisonné is formed by soldering copper wire in desired patterns on to a copper object such as a bowl. The interstices are then filled several times with enamel and baked, before being polished and painted.

The cut-out maker who made stencils of fine paper, sometimes red and sometimes in other colours
and in a multitude of patterns, for use as home and window decorations.

The cut-out maker worked by eye and memory, cutting several sheets of paper at one time.

Sign-board for a carpet shop.

A carpet weaver at work.

Spinning silk floss into thread. This was done out-of-doors, the thread being
twisted to impart additional strength by rotating the metal balls suspended from one end
which are to be seen below the operator's left hand.

Silk embroidery, painstaking work of great delicacy. The finest work was done by men. In imperial China most official clothing was elaborately embroidered.

Beating raw cotton to remove the dust and fibres.

Hand-spinning cotton thread.

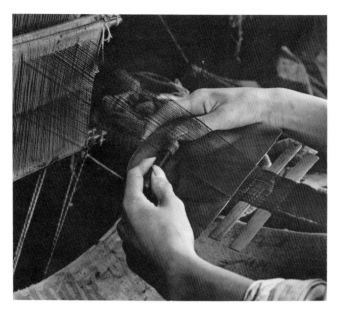

Weaving ankle bands to secure the bottoms of trouser legs.

Embroidering a child's cotton apron with cross stitch.

Pewter was used in the manufacture of many household utensils.

Paper making by the traditional method, similar to that used when the process was
first invented in China. The difference was that the raw material was ground up
rags and recycled paper and the end product a very coarse one. The
raw material was ground up and reduced to a slurry from which sheets
of paper particles were dipped out on a bamboo frame.

Pasting up paper sheets to dry.

Wire making, a process used for silver, copper and brass. The metal was hammered out
into lengths roughly the diameter of a little finger. At one end it would be hammered out
into a much finer wire, fed through a hole in an iron die and attached to
the hand-operated windlass. The wire would be forced through the die and the process repeated
with smaller holes in the die until the desired diameter was achieved.

Casting iron cooking pots at foundries to the west of Peking.

To the west of Peking were to be found ancient tile kilns where
both household and ornamental tiles were still being produced.

Kilns supplied the materials necessary for the restoration of temples and palaces.

Hand-planing the body of a Chinese fiddle.

A tape measure made from a solid piece of hardwood carved and studded with brass and with functional but ornamental iron work.

Drilling holes in the side of a *man-t'ou* steaming basket with one of the
old-fashioned hand tools which were still in use in Peking.

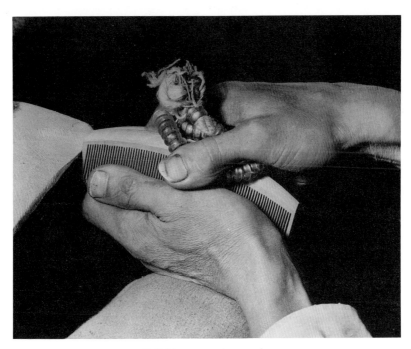

Polishing a wooden comb.

People were never idle: these old women were making small straw toy figures.
The women's feet were bound, a cruel custom which was universal among Chinese,
but not Manchu, women in Manchu China.

Further Afield

BEYOND the immediate environs of Peking most of the important local sites of old China lay to the west or north where the North China plain gives way to mountain ranges. Piercing the ranges and giving access to Mongolia was the Nan K'ou pass, a defile of vital strategic importance. At the far end of the pass lay the Great Wall which extended from there to the sea in one direction and far into western China in the other. It could be reached by rail and then explored on foot. On one visit I left an exposed film behind on the wall and only discovered the loss after my return to the railway station. I went back to fetch it and had to spend a chilly night in one of the watch-towers.

The hills were sadly bare as the original tree cover had long been destroyed. The poverty of the peasants meant that anything combustible was collected for fuel. No bush could achieve any size before it was cut down and even rank grass and other herbage was ripped up and carried away to the villages. Some trees were grown on private land but the only substantial trees to be seen grew where they were protected, especially around the temples.

East of Nan K'ou, standing in lonely grandeur on a bare plain lying up against the hills, were the thirteen Ming tombs. Visitors would generally take a train to Nan K'ou and hire donkeys for the journey. Archaeologists of the People's Republic have excavated one of the main tombs and recovered a fabulous treasure of beautiful objects that were buried with the Wan Li Emperor who died in 1620. The other tombs have yet to be excavated.

Most of the temples of the Western Hills were Buddhist. They were of considerable religious importance and were the destinations of pilgrimage by the devout which contributed to the temple finances and helped to provide maintenance. In the past the temples had also received much imperial patronage, especially during the reign of Ch'ien Lung. The most sacred of the sites was Miao Feng Shan (the Mountain of the Spiritual Peak) south-west of Nan K'ou. It was dedicated to Kuan Yin, the Goddess of Mercy. There was a great spring pilgrimage here during the first half of the fourth moon which was of special significance to women. The pilgrimage was well organized, various benevolent societies providing shelter and refreshments along the way, a long, stony five-hour walk. Donkeys and sedan chairs were available for those who could not manage the walk. It was a particularly happy and joyous occasion.

Far to the south in the further Western Hills were two great temples in particularly fine surroundings. These were T'an Che Ssu (the Monastery of Clear Pools and Wild Mulberry) and Chieh T'ai Ssu (the Ordination Terrace Temple). The former was situated in a prettily wooded valley, the latter high up on a ridge top. A feature of these and almost all other

211

temples were the fine trees growing in the temple precincts, mainly ginkgo trees and pines. Some of the pines were an especially beautiful species with silvery white bark.

I visited T'an Che Ssu and Chieh T'ai Ssu on several occasions, the most memorable being the time when I walked to T'an Che Ssu by moonlight. With a friend I walked up from the railway station, the moon so brilliant in the clear north China air that walking was easy. We reached the temple at first light when the monks were just about to commence their first observances for the day. They were surprised to see us at such an hour but made us most welcome and gave us tea and steamed buns. It was always so. I never carried food with me when visiting such temples. I accepted the hospitality and always responded with a silver dollar which was the most acceptable gift in country areas. It was the tradition of Buddhist monks to provide hospitality for travellers. Recollections of the peace and tranquillity of temples in country places with the harmonious sound of bells and chanting and the gracious hospitality of the monks are among my most cherished memories of China.

I paid many visits to the Western Hills, often by myself. Once in winter I lost the way and was kindly sheltered by the monks of one small temple. They were concerned for my well-being and when I left the next morning they insisted on my wrapping some old newspapers around my legs to keep them warm.

My longest visit to the Western Hills took place in 1936 when I visited a group of people living over one hundred kilometres west of Peking just beyond a gate known as Ta Lung Men through a spur of the Great Wall. Known to foreigners as the Lost Tribe, they were the descendants of followers of the rebel chief Li Tzu Ch'eng, who captured Peking in 1643. When Li was driven out of Peking by the Manchus his followers fled to the Western Hills. Here they eventually made their submission and were allowed to settle in the Lost Tribe area. It was a poor district, lacking in historical monuments, and the people were singularly unchanged. I saw no hint of Western influence in the area. The main economic activity was the manufacture of incense. I went there with three donkeymen and three donkeys and was very well cared for. Every evening I settled my account with the head donkeyman, making payment from my slender store of silver dollars.

In many of the temples closer to Peking foreigners used to rent courtyards for use as weekend residences. One of the finest and best-known of these was Pi Yün Ssu (the Temple of the Azure Clouds). This consisted of a succession of fine halls and courtyards leading up to a square stone tower topped with seven stupas in the Indian style. The halls contained many figures of Buddhist saints. The body of Dr Sun Yat Sen was kept at Pi Yün Ssu for several years before being finally interred in Nanking. Not far from Pi Yün Ssu was Wo Fo Ssu, beautifully situated over a clear stream, where there was a great bronze figure of the reclining Buddha fifteen metres in length. There was also a smaller and older wooden reclining Buddha made from sandalwood, the precious fragrant wood that came from India and the drier parts of South-east Asia. The temple itself dated from the seventh century AD. These temples had often been visited by the emperors and contained many imperial relics.

Over the hills to the south of Pi Yün Ssu was Pa Ta Ch'u, a succession of eight temples running up a valley. This had been a popular summer resort for Europeans. Beyond Pa Ta Ch'u was the interesting T'ien T'ai Ssu (the Temple of the Exalted Heaven) which contained a curious figure said by the monks to be the mummy of the first Manchu emperor, Shun Chih. It was probably neither a mummy nor Shun Chih but the statue of a monk. Nevertheless the legend brought many visitors to the temple which prospered accordingly.

One of the most interesting temples in the hills was Fa Hai Ssu (the Law Ocean Temple) south of Pa Ta Ch'u. It was only a small though very picturesque temple but was remarkable for its fine Ming dynasty frescos. These were on the walls of the main hall and, having been perpetually in the shade, were in a fine state of preservation. When they were being painted some of the roof tiles must have been removed to provide a good light.

In the foothills were two beautiful places which featured springs of crystal clear water. To the north was Hei Lung T'an (the Black Dragon Pool), which lay at the base of a small hill, the pool surrounded by an elegant gallery. At the top of the hill was the shrine of the Dragon King, a powerful deity controlling rainfall. The villagers believed that when the pool bubbled and mist formed on the surface it was a certain indication that rain could be expected. In such a dry place as north China this association with a rain deity was of great local importance. The shrine was an ancient foundation and notable for the fact that during a severe drought in 1725 the emperor sent high officials here to offer prayers. The prayers were answered for rain fell heavily. An honorific tablet was consequently erected with characters reading, 'The Glorious and Divine Spirit that Fertilizes the Earth with Seasonable Showers'.

Further south was the much larger Jade Fountain where another never-failing spring formed a charming pool. This was the source of the water that was channelled into Peking to fill the lakes in the Tartar City. On their way the waters were used to irrigate extensive rice crops between the Jade Fountain and the nearby Summer Palace, one of the few rice-producing areas of north China, and to provide water for the lake in the Summer Palace. In the hill above the pool were several grottoes containing stone figures which had unfortunately been much defaced. Crowning the hill was a splendid pagoda from which a fine view could be obtained over the countryside, and two smaller pagodas.

The Jade Fountain had been a popular pleasure resort of the early Manchu emperors but fell into disrepair in the nineteenth century. The Empress Dowager had thoughts of restoring the whole park, but as this would have been very costly she was persuaded instead to build the Summer Palace next door. This, however, was also a very costly operation largely undertaken with funds intended for the modernization of the Chinese Navy.

The Summer Palace, known to the Chinese as I Ho Yüan (the Park of Peace and Harmony in Old Age), was an ancient park but the buildings in it were largely destroyed by Anglo-French forces in 1860 at the same time as the destruction of the old Summer Palace a few kilometres away. Large-scale restoration began in 1889. The Empress Dowager was extremely fond of the place and spent as much time there as possible. But the irresponsible manner of its financing was disastrous for China and accounted at least in part for the easy Japanese victory in the war of 1894.

A steep hill capped by a four-storey tower containing a large gilt figure of the Goddess of Mercy overlooked the large lake. On the northern and eastern sides of the lake stood many halls and pavilions and a large theatre. Although the architecture was not as refined as that of the older buildings in and around Peking, the Summer Palace was nevertheless picturesque. The camel-back bridges on the western side of the lake were especially graceful.

The old Summer Palace, Yüan Ming Yüan, which was replaced by I Ho Yüan, was some kilometres to the north-west of the latter. Built on a lavish scale in the eighteenth century it displayed many features derived from European architecture of the time, the Emperor Ch'ien Lung having been impressed by accounts given to him of the Palace of Versailles. It did not, however, have a long life for it was sacked and burned down in 1860 by British and French forces. This was the final act in a discreditable war which arose because of British and French pressures to obtain greater access to China, extend trade, open embassies in Peking, and legalize opium (a trade item of great importance to the government of British India). These demands were forced on China by an agreement concluded in 1858 but hostilities broke out afresh in 1860 when the Chinese refused to have ratification take place in Peking, demanding instead that it take place in Shanghai. A joint Anglo-French expeditionary force captured Peking. The Yüan Ming Yüan was destroyed as a reprisal for the cruel killing of a British party captured during a truce. There was little to be seen of the old

Summer Palace when I was in Peking. The extensive ruins that remained after 1860 had largely been torn down over the years and used as a source of building materials.

To the south of the Summer Palace was to be found another important group of relics of the old China. In the village of Pa Li Chuang there still stood a magnificent thirteen-storey pagoda erected in 1578. This was all that remained of the once important Tz'u Shou Ssu (the Temple of Compassionate Old Age). Nearby was a cemetery for eunuchs which used to contain the graves of 1,700 important eunuchs of the Ming and Manchu periods. In front of each grave was a stone monolith inscribed with details of the deceased.

A little way to the north was a temple, with a considerable endowment of land, known as Hu Kuo Pao Chung Tzu (the Ancestral Hall of the Exalted, Brave and Loyal), which had been built by the Ming Emperor Yung Lo to honour the memory of a distinguished soldier called Kang T'ieh. During one of Yung Lo's absences from the capital Kang T'ieh was left in charge of the palace. Knowing that his enemies at court would certainly accuse him of having enjoyed improper relations with ladies of the palace during the Emperor's absence, Kang T'ieh demonstrated his loyalty by the somewhat extreme step of having himself castrated. Thus, when the inevitable accusations were made, Kang was able to demonstrate his innocence in no uncertain way. The temple contained a fine figure of Kang T'ieh. A number of eunuchs retired to this temple in 1911, and there were still a number of them there when I was in Peking. They were friendly and hospitable old people, always happy to show visitors around their temple.

A few kilometres further south was the famous Lu Kou Ch'iao, the bridge known to foreigners as the Marco Polo Bridge because the original, built in the twelfth century, was described by that great Venetian traveller. The bridge that he knew was eventually destroyed in a flood but was replaced in the seventeenth century by the present beautiful and splendidly engineered structure. It is a wide stone bridge of eleven arches with marble balustrades, each balustrade pillar topped by the figure of a lion. It was near here in 1937 that an incident contrived by the Japanese sparked off the Japanese attempt to subjugate China which came to an ignominious end in 1945.

The places mentioned in this chapter are only a few of the more important historical locations near Peking. There were many more; some temples were in good repair, but many relics and, in particular, many important tombs had fallen into decay. However, because they were so well built, there were still remnants to be seen by the enquiring visitor interested in China's past.

The splendid marble *p'ai-lou* erected in 1541, to some people the finest in all China,
which stands at the entrance to the Ming tombs.

Beyond the *p'ai-lou* was the entrance gate proper leading to the Tablet House which contained
a great stone monolith standing on the back of a tortoise. This in turn led to the Triumphal
Way, an avenue lined with eighteen pairs of stone figures each carved from a single block of
stone. In the valley beyond were the tombs themselves. Nowadays the whole area is well wooded
but the vastness of the layout was perhaps best gauged in these treeless days before
the revolution of 1949 when trees survived only in the actual tomb precincts.

The Great Wall near the Nan K'ou pass, the narrow defile that gave access to
the plains of Mongolia. The wall stretched over three thousand kilometres
from the sea to the far north-west of China. It never provided
total protection from invasion but had its uses as an early warning system.

Miao Feng Shan (the Mountain of the Spiritual Peak) was the most popular place for pilgrimage by devout Buddhists in the Peking area. The goddess of the temple on the summit was probably a manifestation of the Goddess of Mercy who was credited with many miracles and acts of benevolence. The great annual pilgrimage took place in the spring during the first half of the fourth moon.

Young girl pilgrim on Miao Feng Shan. The pilgrimage was not only a devout but also a very gay occasion in which whole families took part.

A group of monks enjoying a hearty vegetarian meal on Miao Feng Shan.

Chieh T'ai Ssu (the Ordination Terrace Temple), an especially beautiful temple dating originally from the seventh century but frequently rebuilt since that time. It was a favoured resort of the Emperor Ch'ien Lung.

Monk at his devotions in Chieh T'ai Ssu.

T'an Che Ssu (the Monastery of Clear Pools and Wild Mulberry),
another famous temple not far from Chieh T'ai Ssu.

A visitor to T'an Che Ssu bathing his eyes in supposedly curative water from a temple spring.

Some temple statues in the Western Hills. Every temple had
its own images which were the objects of veneration.

Pi Yün Ssu (the Temple of the Azure Clouds), an Indian-style Buddhist temple in the Western Hills. The great marble stupa, built in the reign of Ch'ien Lung, dominates the valley.

The entrance to Pi Yün Ssu.

Wo Fo Ssu (the Temple of the Sleeping Buddha), near Pi Yün Ssu. The bronze image
of the Buddha, fifteen metres in length, was cast in the fifteenth century.

The Abbot of Sheng Mi Chih T'ang, one of the many temples at which I stayed.
The Abbot was a courteous, kindly man who made visitors welcome.

The pattern of fields in spring seen from the hillock of the Black Dragon Pool.

The entrance to the Black Dragon Pool, a fine never-failing spring of water on
an outlier of the Western Hills and by tradition believed to be the home of a benevolent dragon
which could be depended on to help end serious droughts in the region.

Ta Chüeh Ssu, a tranquil temple where springs issued from
the foothills, a place notable for its ancient trees.

Pewter altarware at Ta Chüeh Ssu.

An elaborate chime at Ta Chüeh Ssu.

Pagodas at the Jade Fountain, just to the west of the Summer Palace.

Winter morning at the Jade Fountain with mist on the surface of the
pool that never freezes, the source of the stream feeding the Peking lakes.

Camel-back bridge at the Summer Palace.

The same camel-back bridge from across the Palace Lake. Although
the Summer Palace is an ancient site, the present buildings were built by the Empress Dowager
largely with funds intended for the modernization of the Chinese navy in the 1890s.

The Summer Palace after snowfall. Snow rarely falls in Peking and does not last long.

The Summer Palace seen from the summit of the main Jade Fountain Pagoda. The perpetual flow of water from the Jade Fountain irrigated an area of rice fields which are rare in north China.

A simple country flour mill.

Lunch pause during harvest.

Planting out rice seedlings.

Watering radishes by hand.

A sheltered nursery bed for vegetable seedlings.

Fa Hai Ssu (the Law Ocean Temple), a small temple in the Western Hills which
was remarkable for its Ming frescos still in an excellent state of preservation. The walls
on which they had been painted were always in near darkness.

The Eunuchs' Temple, built in honour of a distinguished Ming soldier, Kang T'ieh, who had himself castrated so that he could not be accused of dishonouring the emperor when left in charge of the palace.

Statue of Kang T'ieh.

One of the old palace eunuchs who had retired to the temple
when China became a republic in 1912.

A view to the hills from within the Eunuchs' Temple precincts.

A wayside shrine still well maintained by neighbouring farmers.

The thirteen-storey Pa Li Chuang pagoda, built in 1578 and originally part
of a large temple complex, most of which had disappeared.

A loaded camel train on its way to Peking. When you bought your fuel
for the winter you were likely to find the *hu-t'ung* outside your door filled
with solemn seated camels philosophically chewing the cud.

The approach to Lu Kou Ch'iao (the Marco Polo Bridge).

Lu Kou Ch'iao, which was the scene of the incident in 1937 engineered by
the Japanese as a pretext for their massive invasion of China. The bridge is on the
same site as that described by Marco Polo, which was washed away in the seventeenth century.

Postscript

After my departure from Peking in 1946 I returned briefly in 1948 to collect some belongings. Thirty years were then to pass before I saw the city again, in 1979 and 1982. The changes that had taken place were enormous. The Peking that I knew is now no more than the core of a huge metropolis spreading out in every direction to cover what used to be agricultural land. There has been large-scale industrialization and nowadays when you look out from cherished viewpoints of times past you see a panorama of innumerable multi-storey buildings punctuated by tall factory chimneys belching smoke. The splendid city walls have been razed and the moat filled in to provide room for a ring road. The brilliant north China light has lost its shine to a layer of smog.

Many of the famous relics of the imperial past have been well cared for and the interest of the Chinese public in them is evident from the crowds of Chinese visitors. But many places that I knew well are no longer accessible to the public, notably Chung Hai, Nan Hai and the Jade Fountain. Some buildings have been demolished and some converted to other uses.

One can appreciate the problems of conservation. China, despite its size, is not a rich country, and there must be a limit to the resources that the new China can devote to maintaining the enormous cultural heritage that has come down to it from the old.

Change had to come and I have no doubt that the people are today infinitely better off and live under a much fairer system than when I resided in Peking. In Peking, as everywhere else that I visited, a modest measure of affluence was evident. People were cheerful, well fed and well clothed. And it was obvious, to judge from the well-patronized restaurants and the fine food to be had in them, that the Chinese have retained their traditional appreciation of good cooking.

One may easily question whether it was a good thing to allow the city to grow to its present enormous size and to permit the establishment of so much industry there, given the dryness of the area, and whether more imaginative planning might not have saved at least part of the walls. Despite this Peking remains one of the world's great cities.

The years that I spent in Peking were formative ones and I am grateful that I was privileged to catch a glimpse of a bygone China that had good sides as well as bad ones and which has now gone forever.

Bibliography

Many books have been written about Peking and outstanding are *In Search of Old Peking* by L.C. Arlington and William Lewisohn and *The Adventures of Wu* by H.Y. Lowe. Arlington, an American, was an old-timer, having arrived in China in 1879 where he served in the customs and postal administrations. Lewisohn was a former regular British Army officer who became a journalist. Their work is authoritative, concise, highly informative and written in a most lively style. Originally published by Henry Vetch in 1935, *In Search of Old Peking* was reprinted by Paragon Book Reprint Corporation of New York in 1967. It should be noted that the map was reprinted separately.

H.Y. Lowe was a native Pekingese who spent some time in America. He was encouraged to write by Edgar Snow. His work appeared in instalments in the *Peking Chronicle*, and was published in book form as *The Adventures of Wu* in two volumes in 1940 and 1941. It was reprinted by the Princeton University Press in 1983, complete with an index and an introduction by Professor Derk Bodde. It is a gentle, charming account of the life cycle of a young man from a well-to-do Peking family from birth to marriage in the nineteen twenties and thirties. The account is rose-tinted but contains a wealth of information on tradition and custom. At the end of the Pacific War Lowe had a curio shop in Peking. What happened to him after the Communist takeover is not known.

Juliet Bredon's *Peking*, containing less information and much more sentiment, is a useful complement to Arlington and Lewisohn. *The Moon Year* by Bredon and Mitrophanow is a valuable account of the Chinese calendar and the activities that took place during the year. Both works have been reprinted by the Oxford University Press. For those who wish to know more there is *Annual Customs and Festivals in Peking*, Derk Bodde's translation of a work by a Manchu official, reprinted by the Hong Kong University Press in 1965.

Chinese Creeds and Customs by Colonel V.R. Burckhardt is a glossy Hong Kong compilation derived from three earlier volumes and published in 1982, fourteen years after the Colonel's death. Its purview is by no means confined to south China for Colonel Burckhardt was a China specialist with many years' service in China, much of it spent in Peking. He had a life-long interest in the subject of the book.

I have referred with benefit to two small guide books which appeared at the end of the Pacific War. One was produced by Henry Vetch, the other was a compilation organized by Margaret Lea of the American Red Cross and containing excellent material by authoritative writers including H.Y. Lowe.

Mr Lewisohn's route book and map, *The Western Hills of Peking*, published by Henry

Vetch in 1933, makes nostalgic reading today. The 1965 work *Peking* by Nigel Cameron and Brian Brake (the distinguished New Zealand photographer) is a beautiful book and provides a notable photographic record of Peking on the eve of the Cultural Revolution.

Perceptive memoirs of Peking in the thirties by three well-qualified observers are: *The Years That Were Fat* by George Kates, the relevant chapters of *Memoirs of an Aesthete* by Harold Acton, and *City of Lingering Splendour* by John Blofeld. Novels of the good life in Peking as viewed from the British Embassy are Anne Bridge's *Peking Picnic* and *The Ginger Griffin*.

For some understanding of the harsh underside of Peking life one should read Lao She's *Rickshaw*, translated by Jean M. James and published by the University of Hawaii Press in 1979.

For furniture see *Chinese Household Furniture* by George Kates, published in 1948; a Dover paperback appeared in 1962. The best concise work on Chinese symbols is in German, Wolfram Eberhard's *Lexikon Chinesische Symbole*, published by Eugen Diederichs in 1983. A simpler work is *A Sketch of Chinese Arts and Crafts* by Hilda Strong, the third edition of which was published by Henry Vetch in 1933. Miss Bieber's toggles are described in *Substance and Symbol in Chinese Toggles* by Schuyler Cammann, published in 1962 by the University of Pennsylvania Press.

An interesting short account of Chinese food and dinner party customs is contained in *The Chinese Festive Board* by Corrinne Lamb, originally published by Henry Vetch in Peking and reprinted by Vetch and Lee in Hong Kong in 1970.

There are various works on the theatre. A good introduction to the subject is Arlington and Acton's *Famous Chinese Plays*, published by Vetch in 1937.

For general background the learned and unlearned alike cannot do better than turn to the recently published *Cambridge Encyclopaedia of China*, a remarkable one-volume distillation of an enormous range of subject-matter by an impressive list of contributors. The *Encyclopaedia Sinica*, published in Shanghai in 1917 and reprinted by the Oxford University Press, is in no way comparable but still contains many items of interest not to be found in the later work.

For technology a very interesting book is *China at Work* by Rudolf P. Hommel, published by John Day in New York in 1937. The research for the book was undertaken mainly in central China but its account of the often simple tools and techniques with which Chinese workers achieved such remarkable results is of direct relevance to what I saw in Peking.

Romanization

THE romanization of the Chinese language, which is monosyllabic and tonal, is fraught with problems. The situation has been complicated by the existence of a bewildering number of romanization systems. Every important nation establishing relations with China in the past has introduced its own system designed to reflect the pronunication of its own language. Moreover, sinologists in a number of countries have been zealous in devising their own systems. Thus the British, the French, the German, the Dutch, the Swedes, and many other nationalities all have their own system or several systems of romanization. Many writers and journalists did not trouble to follow a system with any degree of consistency, thus perpetuating a number of romanized forms of hybrid derivation. In rendering their own names into English, the Chinese themselves, to whom the idea of romanized Chinese was curious if not bizarre, have introduced some forms that owe no allegiance to any system but reflect dialect idiosyncracies.

The system in most common use in English-language publications until fairly recently was the Wade-Giles system and, with one or two exceptions, this is the system used in *A Photographer in Old Peking*. (Notable among the exceptions are 'Sun Yat Sen' and 'Chiang Kai Shek', aberrant romanized forms which are so universally followed that it would create further confusion to change them.) For the names of provinces, cities and towns, I have used the so-called Post Office system, as it was the system used in most English-language maps and atlases of China published in the first decades of this century.

Given below is a list of the names and terms as they appear in the pages of this book, the Chinese characters in their full (that is, unsimplified) form, and their equivalents in the Pinyin system. That system was devised in the People's Republic of China, and since its official adoption has been the standard romanization in English-language works published in China, and has been gaining increasing acceptance in English works on Chinese subjects published in other parts of the world.

An Ting Men	安定門	Andingmen
Ch'ang An Chieh	長安街	Changanjie
Ch'eng Huang Miao	城隍廟	Chenghuangmiao
Ch'i Nien Tien	祈年殿	Qiniandian
Ch'i Pai Shih	齊白石	Qi Baishi
Chiang Kai Shek	蔣介石	(unchanged)

chiao-tzu	餃子	*jiaozi*
Chieh T'ai Ssu	戒台寺	Jietaisi
Ch'ien Lung	乾隆	Qianlong
Ch'ien Men	前門	Qianmen
Ch'ing Ming	清明	Qingming
Ch'ü Fu	曲阜	Qufu
Chung Hai	中海	Zhonghai
Fa Hai Ssu	法海寺	Fahaisi
feng-shui	風水	*fengshui*
Ha Ta Men	哈達門	Hadamen
Hei Lung T'an	黑龍潭	Heilongtan
Hsi Chih Men	西直門	Xizhimen
Hsi Yü Ssu	西峪寺	Xiyusi
Hsiang Fei	香妃	Xiang Fei
Hu Kuo Pao Chung Tzu	護國褒忠祠	Huguobaozhongzi
hu-t'ung	胡同	*hutong*
hua-mei	畫眉	*huamei*
hua-piao	華表	*huabiao*
Hua Shan	華山	Huashan
Huang Fei Hu	黃飛虎	Huang Feihu
Hui	回	Hui
I Ho Yüan	頤和園	Yiheyuan
Jehol, now referred to as Ch'eng Te	熱河承德	Chengde
k'ang	坑	*kang*
Kang T'ieh	剛鐵	Gang Tie
Kansu	甘肅	Gansu
Kuan Yin	觀音	Guanyin
Kuang Hsü	光緒	Guangxi
K'ung Miao	孔廟	Kungmiao
kuo-t'ieh	鍋貼	*guotie*
Lao She	老舍	Lao She
Lao Tzu	老子	Laozi

Li Tzu Ch'eng	李自成	Li Zicheng
ling-chih	靈芝	*lingzhi*
Liu Li Ch'ang	琉璃廠	Liulichang
Lu Kou Ch'iao	蘆溝橋	Lugouqiao
Lung Fu Ssu	隆福寺	Longfusi
ma-ping	麻餅	*mabing*
man-t'ou	饅頭	*mantou*
Men T'ou Kou	門頭溝	Mentougou
Miao Feng Shan	妙峯山	Miaofengshan
Nan Ch'ang Chieh	南長街	Nanchangjie
Nan Hai	南海	Nanhai
Nan K'ou	南口	Nankou
Nanking	南京	Nanjing
Ninghsia	寧夏	Ningxia
Niu Jou Wan	牛肉宛	Niurouwan
Pa Kua	八卦	Bagua
Pa Li Chuang	八里莊	Balizhuang
Pa Ta Ch'u	八大處	Badachu
pai-kan	白乾	*baigan*
pai-ling	百靈	*bailing*
p'ai-lou	牌樓	*pailou*
Pai T'a Ssu	白塔寺	Baitasi
Pai Yün Kuan	白雲觀	Baiyunguan
pao-tzu	飽子	*baozi*
Pei Hai	北海	Beihai
Peking	北京	Beijing
Pi Yün Ssu	碧雲寺	Biyunsi
Shansi	山西	Shanxi
Shantung	山東	Shandong
Sha Kuo Chü	沙鍋居	Shaguoju
shao-ping	燒餅	*shaobing*
Shao Hsing	紹興	Shaoxing
Shensi	陝西	Shaanxi

Shun Chih	順治	Shunzhi
Sinkiang	新疆	Xinjiang
Soochow	蘇州	Suzhou
Sun Wu K'ung	孫悟空	Sun Wukong
Sun Yat Sen	孫逸仙	(unchanged)
Szechuan	四川	Sichuan
Ta Chüeh Ssu	大覺寺	Dajuesi
Ta Chung Ssu	大鍾寺	Dazhongsi
Ta Fo Ssu	大佛寺	Dafosi
Ta Hui Ssu	大慧寺	Dahuisi
Ta Lung Men	大龍門	Dalongmen
t'ai-chi	太極	*taiji*
T'ai Ho Men	太和門	Taihemen
T'ai Ho Tien	太和殿	Taihedian
T'ai Miao	太廟	Taimiao
T'ai P'ing	太平	Taiping
T'ai Shan	泰山	Taishan
T'an Che Ssu	潭柘寺	Tanzhesi
Taoism	道教	Daoism
Ti T'an	地壇	Ditan
T'ien An Men	天安門	Tiananmen
T'ien Ch'iao	天橋	Tianqiao
T'ien Ning Ssu	天寧寺	Tianningsi
T'ien T'ai Ssu	天台寺	Tiantaisi
Tientsin	天津	Tianjin
Ts'an T'an	蠶壇	Cantan
Tsingtao	青島	Qingdao
Tung An Shih Ch'ang	東安市場	Donganshichang
Tung Pien Men	東便門	Dongbianmen
Tung Yüeh Miao	東岳廟	Dongyuemiao
Tz'u Shou Ssu	慈壽寺	Cishousi
Wan Li	萬曆	Wanli
Wang Ch'ing Fang	王青芳	Wang Qingfang

Wang Fu Ching Ta Chieh	王府井大街	Wangfujingdajie
Wei Hai Wei	威海衛	Weihaiwei
Wo Fo Ssu	卧佛寺	Wofosi
Wu Men	午門	Wumen
Wu T'a Ssu	五塔寺	Wutasi
Yang	陽	Yang
yang-ch'e	洋車	*yangche*
Yangtzu	揚子	Yangzi
Yin	陰	Yin
Yüan Ming Yüan	圓明園	Yuanmingyuan
Yün Kang	雲岡	Yungang
Yung Cheng	雍正	Yongzheng
Yung Ho Kung	雍和宮	Yonghegong
Yung Lo	永樂	Yonglo

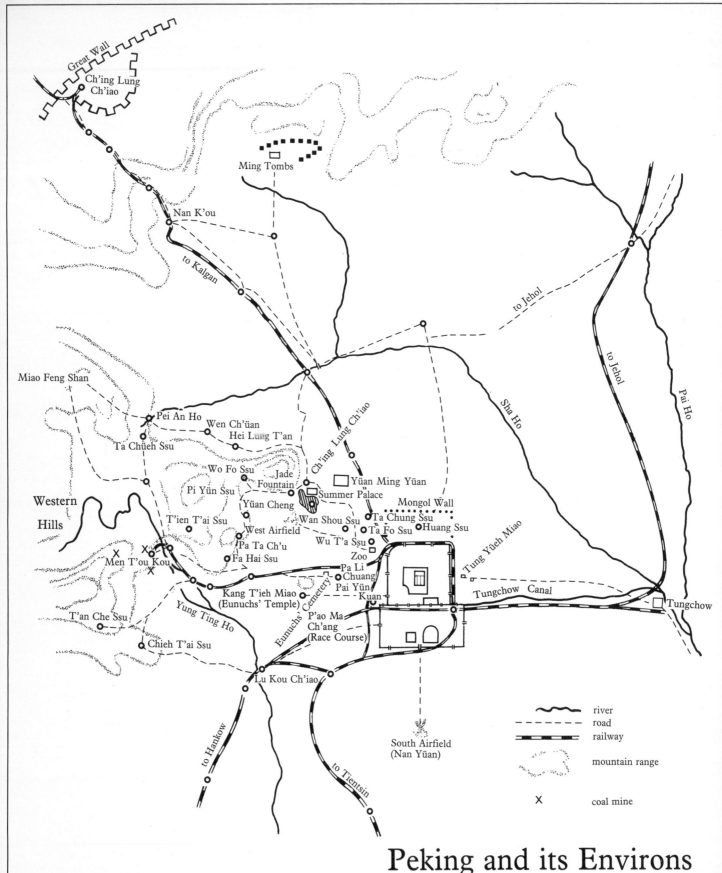

Peking and its Environs

Map labels:

Great Wall
Ch'ing Lung Ch'iao
Ming Tombs
Nan K'ou
to Kalgan
to Jehol
to Jehol
Sha Ho
Pai Ho
Miao Feng Shan
Pei An Ho
Wen Ch'üan
Hei Lung T'an
Ta Chüeh Ssu
Ch'ing Lung Ch'iao
Wo Fo Ssu
Jade Fountain
Yüan Ming Yüan
Pi Yün Ssu
Summer Palace
Yüan Cheng
Mongol Wall
Western Hills
T'ien T'ai Ssu
Wan Shou Ssu
Ta Chung Ssu
West Airfield
Ta Fo Ssu
Huang Ssu
Pa Ta Ch'u
Wu T'a Ssu
Men T'ou Kou
Fa Hai Ssu
Zoo
Tung Yüeh Miao
Pa Li
Chuang
Kang T'ieh Miao
(Eunuchs' Temple)
Pai Yün
Kuan
Eunuchs' Cemetery
Tungchow Canal
Tungchow
T'an Che Ssu
Yung Ting Ho
P'ao Ma
Ch'ang
(Race Course)
Chieh T'ai Ssu
Lu Kou Ch'iao
to Hankow
South Airfield
(Nan Yüan)
to Tientsin

Legend:

river
road
railway
mountain range
X   coal mine